Spring:
THROUGH THE SEASONS

Spring:
THROUGH THE SEASONS

Stories of a Texas Town

Margaret Mallott Smith

FIRST EDITION
Copyright © 2001
By Margaret Mallott Smith
Published in the United States of America
By Sunbelt-Eakin
A Division of Sunbelt Media, Inc.
P.O. Drawer 90159 ⬛ Austin, Texas 78709-0159
email: eakinpub@sig.net
⬛ website: www.eakinpress.com ⬛
ALL RIGHTS RESERVED.

1   2   3   4   5   6   7   8   9
1-57168-611-8 HB
1-57168-613-4 PB

For CIP information, please access:
www.loc.gov

Dedication

This book is dedicated to those
who have done so much to preserve Spring's history:
to **John Robinson** who has collected and shared Spring
memorabilia with a tireless and generous spirit;
to **LuAnne Wunsche Schultz** who led
the Spring Historical Society in the task of
creating the Spring Historical Museum;
to the museum volunteers, especially **Betty Avara**,
for their unswerving service;
without them our work would have been in vain;
and to all my dear friends who shared their stories with me.

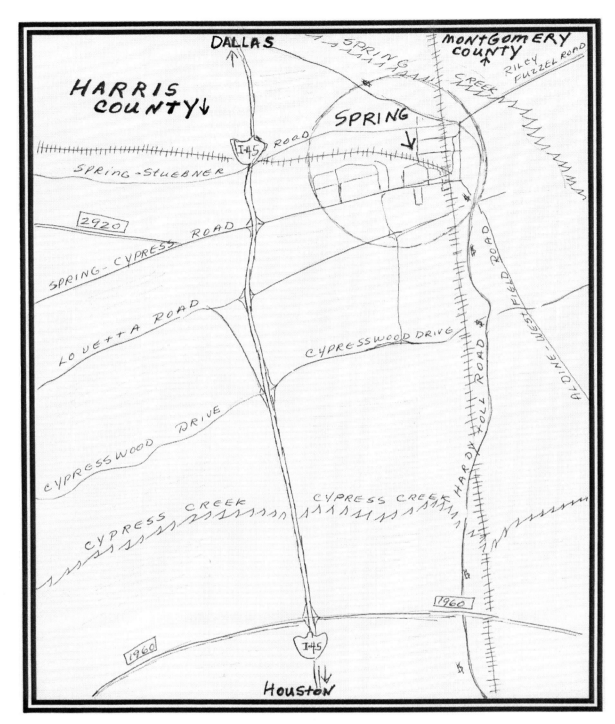

Location of Spring, Texas

Where is Spring, Texas? The tiny town is twenty-five miles north of Houston and two hundred miles south of Dallas. Located in North Harris County, Spring is at the end of Spring-Cypress Road one mile east of Interstate 45 where Hardy Road crosses the railroad tracks. The section on the map enclosed in a rectangle is often called the "Spring area" of Harris County; the actual town is enlarged in the circle on the right. The core of the town is on two streets, Main and Midway, and the accompanying cross streets. As a community, Spring is about 160 years old although pinpointing an exact date of settlement is difficult. Spring is built on a section of the Wiley Smith Survey.

Contents

Comments From a Novice Historian

In accumulating this history of Spring, Texas, I have learned certain lessons about historical research that may help other novice "pursuers of the past." The lessons are simple, but, for me, profound.

I have learned that history "swells and grows." In many cases, just as I finished a section on Spring and felt I had investigated all available material and recorded the salient features about an aspect of Spring's development, I would pick up an article, speak to a person, or read a little more—and find a whole new vista opening that just had to be written down. As Mrs. Gertie Salyers, our "First Lady" of Spring, in her infinite, nonagenarian wisdom declares, "People don't realize there's a lotta history in a small town." Thus, what began as a short document for the Harris County Historical Commission has expanded into what I feel is a comprehensive narrative about this one tiny locale. I must stop somewhere! I know there is more to record about this area of North Harris County, but for the "casual" historian, here is a fast read on a fascinating setting!

From my research, I have learned that history can vary drastically, depending on the source and the point of view. For years, I criticized faulty or skewed histories about my town. (After all, I had lived there, and I knew!) I will be more careful of my criticism, for I have found that even the best sources may be contradictory. What one says is not what another says, and then documentation in the most reliable of materials may say something else. History can indeed be in the eye of the beholder. When contradictions in details occur, I have taken the middle ground. Or, more likely than not, I have

suggested that certain information may be altered by the position of the source, but "here it is all the same."

The final lesson is that one's own perspective can be altered by history—drastically altered. The town of my childhood, I thought, was just a little railroad town that flourished and then declined. While sitting at the knees of the "old-timers," I heard tales that shaped Spring pioneers into a tough breed who wielded the whip, the gun, the fist, the dollar, and the plow with equal dexterity. The frontier was not just Out West; it was here on the streets of Spring. I have come to love these lusty people and their stories. Forgive me if I dwell on their lives too much; I want them to be remembered as much as the development of the town itself is remembered.

In terms of authenticating material: sources are usually identified in the text with a complete list of sources included at the end of the manuscript. In many places where credit is not given to a particular work or person, I, myself, function as the source, citing details that are common knowledge, or my own knowledge.

For those who enjoy the factual side of history, I believe enough is here in document and documentation to validate the origins of the town and its varying facets. For those who enjoy the wonderful tidbits about humanity that one finds in any place or in any person living as long as Spring has, I believe enough is here to please their tastes also.

Thus, *Spring: Through the Seasons—Stories of a Texas Town.*

MARGARET M. SMITH

vii

Spring:
THROUGH THE SEASONS

Stories of a Texas Town

The local newspaper, *The Old Town Spring Souvenir,* reports in a publicity blurb:

> Old Town Spring, Texas, just north of Houston provides one of the most exciting shopping and dining experiences in Texas. This beautifully restored turn-of-the century railroad town contains more than 170 specialty shops, galleries, restaurants, and museums.
>
> Each harkens back to the charm, warmth, and ambiance of down-home memories and fun. Nestled among towering sycamore and pecan trees, the town is justly proud of its reputation as one of the most popular shopping destinations in Texas.

From this description, Old Town Spring sounds delightful, and, indeed, the town is. Visitors from literally all over the world come to Spring to shop and to enjoy the "ambiance of down-home," turn-of-the-[twentieth] century Texas.

But, if we stop a moment—if we stand by the tracks and see the great trains still come roaring by—if we drive over to the ruin of the old sawmill—if we walk in the little, overgrown cemetery tucked back off Aldine-Westfield Road—we find that there is a dimension beyond the "charm, warmth, and ambiance of down-home memories." Instead, we find the vestiges of a gritty little town that once was, seasons ago, vastly different from this pretty place where shoppers play.

The First Traders—Indians in the Spring Creek Area

Before the railroad, before the German farmers, even before the European explorers, there were the Native Americans, the Orcoquisac Indians—hunters and traders who found deer, bear, and buffalo in the Spring Creek woods. The Indians' presence has been noted by archaeological studies that verify the existence of Orcoquisac camps on the banks of the Spring and Cypress Creeks. Carmine Stahl, forester with the Jesse H. Jones Park and Nature Center, which is located near these creek areas, describes fragmented evidence of Indian villages alongside the waterways and tells of Indian trade with French and Spanish explorers as they exchanged "everything from canoes to catfish." Stahl declares that seventeenth century Spanish explorers left "very careful logs and other documents detailing their relationship [with these Indians]."

Remembered for their craftsmanship, The Orcoquiza, numbering about one-thousand members in the tribe, received praise for creating large, dugout canoes and fine, tanned bearskins. Some records indicate that Europeans arrived as early as 1745 when the Orcoquiza were visited by Spanish missionaries. During this time, French traders supposedly came regularly to get bearskins and buckskins from the Indians. By 1756, the Spanish had laid out the Atascosito Trail, an important military and trade route near the area known as Spring, perhaps stimulating the association between Europeans and the Native Americans in the area.

The encroaching Europeans who brought prosperity to the Orcoquiza also brought a deadly disease to the quiet, shy, yet friendly Indians. In an interview with Leslie McDowell, news reporter, Stahl explains that these

1

Atakapan-speaking Indians grouped together in small camps, about two hundred people in a village, and they fared well until the tribe was struck by an epidemic of smallpox which reduced the Orcoquiza to a handful of members. Stahl says, "There were probably 24 [of these Indians] in the area until just after World War I."

According to one story, a part of these dwindling numbers of Orcoquiza lived hidden in the woods near a German family's farm some distance from Spring. For years, the farmer's wife left a loaf of bread on her porch each night for the Indians. The next morning she would find the bread gone, and in its place—a fresh catfish. An extention of the account found in Severance's history, *Deep Roots, Strong Branches*, presents the sad ending of the tale. One day the German farm woman placed the bread on the porch, and the loaf remained there the next day until after sundown. The saddened *Frau* carried the bread back into her house and spoke to her family in German: "The Indians are no more." No trace of the Orcoquiza can be found today. Quite possibly, the few Native Americans who remained in the Spring area relocated on the Indian reservation near Livingston, according to Stahl. However, if we honor this story, the Orcoquiza were traders to the very end!

Points of Controversy

Just as one has to consider the accuracy of the previous account and couch it in "probable" terms, one has to consider carefully the accuracy of some of the other information available about the Spring area in the early 1800s. Two details common to most historical articles on Spring are questionable. Sources tell us that the Texas army camped in the area of Spring Creek near Spring on April 17, 1836, as they marched to San Jacinto. This romantic notion associates Spring with Texas's battle for independence. Little credence can be given to this story since Sam Houston and his army are known to have traveled over the west side of Harris County on their way to San Jacinto.

Also, many historical documents credit William Pierpont, a Connecticut Yankee, with establishing a trading post on Spring Creek in 1838. Sources say that even though Pierpont moved away to Houston, he is the first to leave a permanent record that verifies the beginnings of the Town of Spring. John Robinson, Houston attorney, Spring native, and noted Spring historian himself, challenges this point. Robinson clarifies his remarks by stating that if the history of North Harris County is to be correctly recorded, one must distinguish between the Town of Spring; Spring Creek, Texas; and Spring Creek County. On January 21, 1841, Spring Creek County was created by the State of Texas for judicial and other purposes. Boundaries of the newly created county included parts of Grimes, Montgomery, and Harris Counties. Spring Creek County was named for the creek which ran through its center. The act creating the county named the initial commissioners, one of whom was *William Pierpont*—hence the possible confusion of associating Pierpont with the Town of Spring when he was actually an official with Spring Creek County.

In 1842, Spring Creek County was abolished by a Texas Supreme Court decision which declared judicial counties unconstitutional. On September 12, 1846, a post office named "Crofts Mill," located near Spring Creek, was established to the west of what is now the town of Tomball. The name of the post office was changed on July 19, 1848, to "Spring Creek, Texas." Later the post office name was changed again—to Rosehill. The name "Rosehill" has stayed to the present, given to the area because of the abundance of wild roses on property nearby.

No wonder then that this similarity in names has caused confusion to record keepers and skewed some historical accounts of North Harris County.

German Immigration and Carl Wunsche

Organized German immigration became an important force in the settlement of rural Texas after Texas won its independence from Mexico in 1836. In efforts to attract settlers to the Republic of Texas, homesteading grants were offered to local citizenry as well as to foreign

08-28-1994 ——————————————————————————————— 1:11 pm

Galveston Immigrant Database
Texas Seaport Museum

Ship JOH. DETHARDT   Arrival Quarter 1   Date 1/22/1848   TEXAS

                                          Month Day Year   Destination

Port of Departure BREMEN   Date Departed   /   /

Family Last Name WUNSCH   Origin SAXONY

	Name	Age	Sex	Occupation
1	CARL GOTT.	39	M	WEAVER
2	CHRISTINE	38	F	
3	CARL GOTT.	17	M	
4	AUGUST G.	10	M	
5	ERNST G.	8	M	
6	WILHELM G.	7	M	
7	GOTLIEB	5	F	

Total People 7

Note
INFO. ALSO IN GCGS
Source
NATIONAL ARCHIVES RECORD GROUP 36. MICROCOPY 575, ROLL #3

Citation
INSMF-01

As German immigrants, Carl Gottleib Wunsche, along with his wife and five children, arrived in Galveston on January 2, 1848. On his arrival ticket, Wunsche is listed as a weaver. In the 1850 census, he designates himself as a "farmer." At that point, his family had expanded to include seven children. He, and later his son, became powerful land barons in the Spring area. From Galveston Immigrant Database.

— Courtesy of
LuAnne Wunsche Schultz

On August 11, 1910, Carl Wunsche's son, Carl Gottleib , Jr., and his wife Jane celebrated their golden wedding anniversary with a family reunion. The portrait here which appeared in the Texas Farm and Fireside *shows the couple with their ten children. Titled "The Wunscke Family Reunion at Spring," the article accompanying the picture reads in part:*

"On last Sunday at their home in Spring Mr. and Mrs. Carl Wunsche celebrated their golden wedding anniversary with a family reunion of their ten children, twenty-three grandchildren, ten great-grandchildren and a number of invited friends and neighbors. A barbecue dinner such as can only be gotten up by the old settlers was served on the lawn. Refreshments were served during the afternoon and music [was] by Mr. and Mrs. John Harless and Clint Harless. Interspersed with general good cheer and toasts to the health of Grandpa and Grandma Wunsche were indulged in until a late hour.

"Uncle Cal, as he is familiarly called, was born in Saxon, Germany, October 21, 1831, and came to this country with his parents when he was a lad of 17, settling in this part of Harris County."

Pictured top row: Tom (Bud) Wunsche, Katie Harliss, Allie, Urilda Kothman, Dell, Clementine Hargrave. Bottom row: William (Bill), Mrs. Jane Wunsche, Carl Wunsche, Mary Kelly, Frances Wilson, Charlie.

Carl Wunsche's brood was strong, assertive, and shrewd. Their domineering characters did much to enliven and enrich the developing town of Spring, Texas! Stories of their accomplishments, talents—and idiosyncracies—still delight Spring natives!

immigrants. Texas granted secure property ownership if the homesteader maintained and improved his property once he settled on it. When German immigrants had land, sometimes free—always inexpensive— dangled before their eyes, they could not resist.

The Spring area can trace its agrarian roots back to the period between 1837 and 1850 with the influx of German immigrant farmers who came into the port at Galveston. These settlers, bold enough to leave their homes for a start in the "new world," began an inland trek to places such as New Braunfels and Fredericksburg. There, they planned to homestead—and farm. Perhaps they were following the advice of the editor of the *Morning Star* on January 10, 1840: "The shortest and easiest way to get rich in Texas is to cultivate the soil."

Many Germans never reached their western destinations. Their stories of settlement vary. Some received land grants: in 1840, a German, Wilhelm Lemm, received land from the Republic of Texas under Sam Houston as President. Lemm had migrated from Germany and served in the Civil War. In 1854, he married Henrietta Horn, and they made their home on Wilhelm's 164 acre tract near Spring, located on Hardy Street and still marked by "Lemm Road." Not all merited free land, but those who bought land found acreage in the Spring area was cheap, plentiful,

August G. Wunsche was Carl Wunsche's second son, a boy of ten when the family debarked in Galveston. Pictured here are August's sons, Frank (Franz) Wunsche, Emil Wunsche, and Otto Wunsche. The picture was taken in about 1900.
— Courtesy of August Wunsche

The Morning Star *on January 10, 1840, reported that "the shortest and easiest way to get rich in Texas is to cultivate the soil." German immigrants lived by words such as these: they bought land and farmed. This model farm of Ernest Benignus, just off Kuykendahl Road, with its spacious home, neatly cultivated fields, and numerous outbuildings shows what German industry and thrift could (and did) achieve.*
— Courtesy of John Robinson

German farmers and their wives worked together to succeed, as illustrated by this German couple whose picture was taken in their field. Making a living was a family affair and as soon as children were old enough, they joined their family in the work of the farm.

— Courtesy of John Robinson

and fertile. Just what was "cheap"? In some cases, twenty-five to fifty cents an acre, says John Robinson in *The Joyce Gay Report,* documentary film on the history of Spring. The German farmers planted potatoes, corn, cotton, and other crops on the "cheap" land; and with typical German industry and thrift, the crops and the families flourished. By 1840, reputedly, 153 people were in the area known as Spring.

Among the names of early German settlers were Fischer, Mueller, and von Meuseback. Later, Kaisers, Wunsches, Mittelstaedts, and Goedeckes, among others, were added to the German cadre. Carl Wunsche, a German immigrant who serves as a prime example of these early settlers, did much toward the development

of the Spring area. Carl Wunsche traveled from central Germany to the United States in the mid 1840s. August Wunsche, Carl Wunsche's great grandson, tells that when Wunsche and his family debarked in Galveston, he did not plan a long trip inland. Wunsche felt a great need to find land quickly, land such as he had left in his native Germany. Carl and his son Carl, Jr., "walked up from Galveston"; they walked west over the salt flats and bayou country and came to Spring. At last *here* they found what they were looking for—land like the land of Germany. Carl Wunsche settled his family in Spring, returned to Germany, and came back with more families for the Spring area.

No one with a name resembling Wunsche can be found in the 1840 census in Harris County. However, in the December 21, 1850, census, Carl Gotleib Wincher [sic] is registered, along with his wife and seven children. *Wincher, Wunschke, Wunscher,* and *Wuensche* are among the varied Anglicized spellings of the German name which in its American translation means *wish.* On the census, Wunsche's place of birth is listed as "Germany"; his occupation, "farmer." Wunsche soon surpassed the simple title of a "farmer" and became a land baron by buying up land that was part of the Wylie Smith Survey for as little as ten to twenty-five cents an acre. Wunsche made money farming, and "since land was the only thing to spend money on, Wunsche bought more land," declares August Wunsche. Turning to another land grant, Wunsche bought 2,400 acres of the H. Decrow Survey for $1.00 an acre, says Arthur Bayer, an authority on early land transfers in the area.

Although Germans were the primary immigrants, others also migrated into the Spring area. According to historian Diana Severance, the population became diverse with "immigrants from Louisiana and the postbellum South [who] moved into the farming community." At this time, sugar cane and cotton were the main cash crops. Severance writes: "The town had a sugar mill for syrup making and two cotton gins." At the sugar cane mill, located on Spring Station Road (Spring Cypress Road), workers crushed sorghum cane and made molasses. The prominent location of the mill gave the bend in the road its name: Sugar Mill Curve. The sugar cane mill operated well into the twentieth cen-

One of the early Spring schools around the turn of the twentieth century. Note that the building has no visible windows; the stark front has only hinged doors to break the otherwise plain face. One Spring schoolhouse, perhaps this one, was pulled around the area on skids by oxen, to locate near the largest number of children. These farm children are barefoot; many of the boys have hats and wear overalls or suspenders. The girls have dresses with blouson tops, drop-waisted. The teacher wears a Gibson blouse and gored skirt. We can imagine that the dog in front has accompanied one of the children to school. All in all, the photograph captures a lifestyle of an era long past, but still romantically cherished.

— Courtesy of John Robinson

tury. From the days of his youth, John Robinson—whose father, R. L. Robinson, planned the area that is now Old Town Spring—remembers with nostalgia the making of ribbon cane syrup in the fall:

> The sure method to tell fall had arrived for the Town of Spring was when Bud Wunsche [grandson of the first Carl Wunsche] fired up his sugarcane mill. When sugarcane was cut in the field it was loaded on a wagon and delivered to the mill located on a curve in the road between Old Town Spring and the Houston highway. The cane was crushed in a set of steel wheels up about seven feet from the ground which squeezed the juice out of the stalk. The force behind the mill was a team of mules walking around and around, pulling the drums together. Juice from the mill was transported to cooking vats located about fifty feet from the wheels. A fire of burning wood provided the heat.
>
> As the cane cooked, a green scum formed on top of the juice. Individuals skimmed the top, placing the scum in garbage containers. It took several hours cooking before Bud Wunsche would judge the syrup done. Some people drank the ribbon cane juice. Other filled buckets or jars to have syrup for home use. [Syrup from Bud Wunsche's mill] was the best ribbon cane syrup one could acquire.

For German farmers like Carl Wunsche, cotton and sugar cane were lucrative crops: all the same, vegetable farming remained an important source for revenue.

In one account, Carl Wunsche is given credit for establishing the first school in Spring. Willie Wunsche, another of Carl Wunsche's great grandsons, born June 19, 1892, enjoyed telling stories of his family. Willie says that a schoolmaster was one of the immigrants the Wunsche family brought with them. The Germans built the schoolmaster a log cabin schoolhouse, Spring's first school. John Robinson notes that this one-room structure created in the late 1800's had "wooden windows, held on by leather straps." Maxine Moore in an article "Spring Community is Carved from Wilderness" quotes a former student's recollection of the school:

> It was a box house on blocks. There were no desks. There were seats like church pews, with four or five kids to a seat. The teacher had a table in the front of the room with a coal-oil lamp on it . . . . It was very cold in the winter, and when the shutters were closed it was so dark that the teacher had to light the lamp.

The German schoolmaster taught the children as best he could. They covered the basics—the three R's—with the few textbooks available. The students also learned lifeskills such as farming and surveying. No matter the exact date and place, a school is a school, one of those institutions that marks a true community. Because of enterprising Germans like Wunsche, Spring was on its way to becoming a real town.

The Railroad and the Plan for the Town

As German settlers were moving into Texas, the railroads in Texas were "moving" also. On December 16, 1836, the First Congress of the Republic of Texas "chartered the Texas Rail Road, Navigation and Banking Company to construct railroads," says George Werner in *The Handbook of Texas*. The company—and the plan—collapsed without the creation of a railroad; however, the issues of transporting goods and travel for people remained a great problem in Texas. At last, a twenty-mile segment from Harrisburg (now a part of Houston) to Stafford's Point (now Stafford) opened on September 7, 1853, the first railroad to operate in Texas. After this initial project, other railroads became active. Werner reports that by "the end of 1861 there were nine railroad companies with about 470 miles of track in Texas. Five of the companies were centered in the Houston area. . . ." As part of this boom, in 1866, the Houston Great Northern Railroad Company was commissioned to build a railroad from Houston north to the Red River, a project which began in 1871. That

railroad would be a vital lifeline for the fast-growing coastal area of Texas. That same railroad was to run through the farming area north of Houston and was to hasten dramatically the organization and growth of the community of Spring.

Common belief is that the Town of Spring was named for Spring Creek, the adjacent watershed. Folklore has a more romanticized version of the naming of the town that may or may not be true—this story is that the railroad workers themselves gave Spring its name. Seemingly, the winter during which the workers cleared a right-of-way from Palestine to Houston was one of the worst in the record books. For long periods, the men suffered through freezing rain and snow. In March, the railroad crew camped about three miles south of a wide creek (Spring Creek). The cruel, winter weather gave way to a mild, beautiful spring. In their relief from the burden of winter, the men gratefully named the camp, "Camp Spring." Later, when a post office was established in 1878 [sic], the word "camp" dropped from the usual address, and the town was simply "Spring." However, the railroad, just like a good parent, never forgot the full name of the town, and even today, the railroad still refers to the *stop* or *service area* of Spring as *Camp Spring!*

Possibly, the railroad gave the town its name; the railroad certainly brought organization to the development of the town. Abstract records trace the multiple transfers of properties (that were to become the Town of Spring) from Will Powars to Berry Eulow (February 19, 1861), and from the State to Wiley Smith (March, 5, 1862). On February 9, 1866, A. S. Long acquired the section of the Wiley Smith Survey destined for the Town of Spring. From Long, The Houston Great Northern Railroad Co. purchased forty-one acres on September 1, 1871. Using this purchase, on February 21, 1873, the railroad filed a subdivision plat which laid out the Town of Spring, a sixteen block village, with the blocks measuring 270 feet long by 270 feet wide, just north of the current location of Old Town Spring. The town first developed, including the first depot, at or near the Hardy Street and Caroline Street railroad crossing. John Robinson believes that a man named Clegg owned one of the first businesses—a "business stand across from the first depot in the Town of Spring." Afterward, the railroad sold its Spring subdivision to the Texas Land Company—again according to abstract statistics, on November 11, 1874. The size of the town was reduced from sixteen blocks to a plan for a town of ten blocks, "and that subdivision has never been altered or amended." says Robinson. At the present time, ten lots of that first subdivision are abandoned.

Yes, Spring was the favored child of the railroad as the owners of the "iron horses" nur-

tured the developing town. At one time, the railroad chose Spring as the "waterhole" for trainloads of cattle being shipped by rail. A stock pen was constructed, and cattle were unloaded from the train, fed, and watered with water pumped up from Spring Creek, before reloading. The layover brought train personnel into the local businesses and provided jobs for local laborers. The steam engines of the trains were watered at Spring's water tower; later the water from the railroad's artesian well was used as the town's primary source for water.

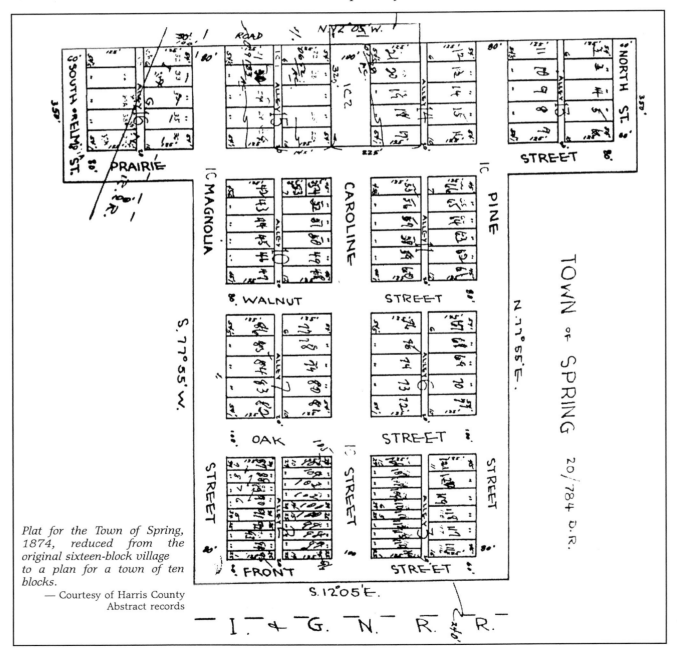

Plat for the Town of Spring, 1874, reduced from the original sixteen-block village to a plan for a town of ten blocks.
— Courtesy of Harris County Abstract records

Contributions of Robert Lee Robinson

In 1902, the present area of Old Town Spring was developed by Robert L. Robinson. John Robinson states, "My father had acquired 40 acres of land from the railroad when he conveyed to the railroad the land where they subsequently built the roundhouse for the railroad . . . My father subdivided the forty acres. This property where Old Town Spring is located is known as the Robinson Addition to the Town of Spring." At the turn of the century, with the establishment of the Fort Worth rail junction,

Spring's depot moved from the Caroline Street crossing to a more convenient location between the two railroad tracks, just across from Robinson's property. Aiding in Robinson's subdivision development, town businesses moved south to the new depot.

The accompanying drawings from the Assessor's Block Book for Harris County, Texas, show the plat of the Town of Spring as laid out by the railroad; the design of the Robinson Addition; the smaller Sellers Addition, which was east of the railroad; and the adjacent Kelly Addition, which sits to the south of the town. The Kelly Addition, on what was originally Wunsche

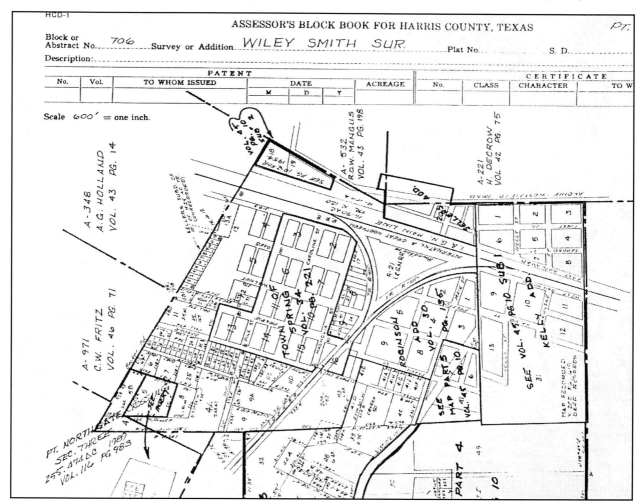

In examining the layers of this drawing from the Assessor's Block Book for Harris County, Texas, one finds the history of land ownership and division (albeit incomplete) of this tiny segment of Texas. The "Town of Spring" and its "Additions" are set on the Wiley Smith Survey. The town is surrounded by the C. W. Fritz, A. G. Holland, R.O.W. Mangus, H. DeCrow, and H. C. Bulrice Surveys. Superimposed on the Smith Survey are the subdivisions: the subdivision plat which laid out the Town of Spring, the Robinson Addition, and the Kelly and Sellers Additions, with street names and block numbers. Divisions and sales of land for commerce, such as Northgate Crossing printed on the map to the north (see bottom left)—are denoted on the Assessor's book. The Houston to Dallas route, not included on this portion of the page, is still labeled "East Montgomery Road" as it was in 1903, with no designation of Hwy. 75 or I-45.

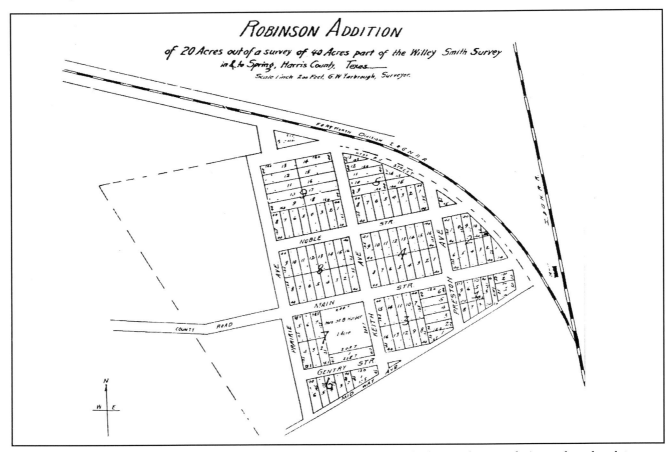

This detail of the Robinson Addition is an enlargement which shows the lots as they are designated on the plat.

land, was named for Irishman M. C. Kelly (Mike), a railroad man, and his wife Mary Jane Wunsche Kelly, one of the daughters of Carl Wunsche, Jr.

Included above is a more detailed drawing of the Robinson Addition "of 20 Acres out of a survey of 40 Acres part of the Willey (sic) Smith Survey in & to Spring, Harris County, Texas." Robinson's declaration to subdivide the forty acres is attached. It reads as follows:

State of Texas
County of Harris

We, R. L. Robinson and wife, Julia E Robinson, being the sole owners of the above described property hereby subdivide the same into blocks and lots, and dedicate the surface rights of Streets and alleys to the ordinary uses of foot passengers and teams.
R. L. Robinson,
Julia E. Robinson.

R. L. Robinson's importance in terms of shaping Spring into a town during the time from 1900 to 1925 cannot be overestimated. His building projects were extensive. As one endeavor, Robinson built what in modern terms would be called a strip center, a group of commercial structures strung together on Main Street next to the railroad track. These buildings were destroyed by fire in 1917. After the fire, Robinson rebuilt the strip center, adding a garage and a building which became the post office. (An *aside:* Ironically, in 1941, these wooden buildings—at that time containing the town post office, a barber shop, and a grocery and feed store—burned also. During the 1970's, a Laundromat on the same property burned. In 1999, a restaurant in Old Town Spring, built on the same site, burned completely. Four fires at the same location! Hot property!) Back to the subject: During these early days, Robinson owned twelve houses and other businesses in addition to the aforementioned strip center.

In the midst of various remodeling and construction projects for the shopping village of Old Town Spring, several of Robinson's first buildings still stand. Three houses on Preston Street, two of which retain the original board and batten siding, were among Robinson's holdings. He also had dwellings on Main Street; one of the most picturesque and unique is the Bradley House on the corner of Keith and Main. A Robinson house moved from Main Street to Midway Street, across from Wunsche Bros. Cafe and Saloon, reputedly had the first in-door commode in Spring, with fixtures installed by Willie Wunsche. The story about the house's plumbing may be true since water was readily available for such use at this home: Robinson provided Spring's first water system, and the house at its original site, was in proximity to the water source that served the town. Today, most of the Robinson houses may be seen in essentially their original external form, although their interiors have been modified to accommodate retail display and sale.

Of course, another modification has come in the changing value of the houses. One long-time Spring resident, Joyce Clairmonte, recalls that in the early 1900's her father rented one of these houses from Mr. Robinson for $10.00 a month, a figure vastly different from Old Town Spring rental property today!

Robert L. Robinson has a list of other credits as a leader in the development of Spring. In terms of business ventures, he developed and operated the aforementioned Spring water system; he served as Depot Agent in Spring for twenty-five years; and he was a produce broker. On May 15, 1899, he shipped the first box car load of potatoes from Spring to the eastern United States market. He continued shipping potatoes until 1936. Since preservation of goods was essential, the railroad built an 8 foot by 8 foot ice box for ice to cool refrigerator cars used to ship Robinson's produce. In 1910, Robinson was a founding member of Spring State Bank. As for community service, he was one of the forerunners in creating the Spring Independent School District in 1907; he was elected to the first board of Trustees of the new school district; he served as a director of the Spring Chamber of Commerce; he donated land to churches and contributed to other charitable causes. Robinson also supported the Spring semi-pro baseball team with a field location on

This house, constructed by R. L. Robinson, has been moved from its locale on Main Street to Gentry Street, across from Wunsche Bros. This cottage is reputedly the first house to have in-door plumbing in Spring.

Robert L. Robinson's far-sighted ventures brought about the creation of Spring in its present location.

— Courtesy of John Robinson

Right: *Pictured here is Elizabeth Ehrhardt Robinson, R. L. Robinson's second wife. Robinson's first wife, Julia Sellers was tragically killed in a car/train accident in 1915. Elizabeth's family, the Ehrhardts, were pioneer settlers in North Harris County, having moved to the area in 1854. Mrs. Robinson's brother, Dr. William Ehrhardt was a doctor in the Bammel-Spring area for over fifty years. Another brother, J. G. Ehrhardt was a County Commissioner in the 1890's.*

The elegance of Mrs. Robinson's attire depicts her elegance. She was a schoolteacher, devoted mother, and church leader. When Mrs. Robinson's son John Marvin went away to college at Southwestern University, Georgetown, Elizabeth Robinson made sure her son was a clean scholar. John dutifully sent his soiled clothes home via the train to Spring. The clothes were laundered and ironed; then Mrs. Robinson put them back on the train to Georgetown and her son! (Another example of the importance of the train to Spring.) For years, Mrs. Robinson served as Sunday School Superintendent at Immanuel Church. She and her husband donated a portion of the land used by the church today.

— Courtesy of John Robinson

Main Street. Only a partial, but overwhelming, list of accomplishments for the "father of Spring," R. L. Robinson.

Property Transactions of J. C. Sellers

R. L. Robinson's father-in-law, J. C. Sellers, was a prosperous and civic-minded gentleman in his own right. As a business man, he established a mercantile store on the corner of Caroline and Hardy Streets in 1890. Just down Hardy Street, he and his family—his wife was the former Julia Pillot, member of a prominent North Harris County family—occupied a classic one-story Victorian home, a show place with accompanying ginger-bread trim and wrap-around porch. Sellers, who had moved in from around Willow Creek, purchased 3,606 acres of land in the Spring area in 1892. The Sellers Addition of Spring lay along the east side of

J. C. Sellers and his wife, the former Julia Pillot, occupied this classic, one-story Victorian home with ornate gingerbread trim. The group on the porch includes R. L. Robinson, Adelle Robinson, Julie E. Sellers, Eugene Robinson, Marie Robinson, and R. L. Robinson's wife Julia.
— Courtesy of John Robinson

the main railroad track. Eventually, a hospital, saloons, and hotels lined Sellers' railroad frontage.

Certain tracts of Sellers' land were further east on Aldine-Westfield Road. A Summation of Sellers's land transactions indicates that this area "incurred a fast development, commencing in 1906" when J. C. and Julia Sellers conveyed land to various parties, land which was used for a variety of commercial and community purposes. On October 4, 1906, J. C. Sellers sold 22.8 acres in the R.O.W. McManus and H. Decrow Surveys to C. G. Barrett, and on this land, which cost $500.00, Barrett built Barrett Saw Mill. On August 15, 1907, Barrett bought more Sellers land—"2.75 acres in the R.O.W. Mc-Manus survey, [a tract] of land known as 'The Old Club Hall and Ground,'" a recreational area for the town. Later in November of the same year, Sellers sold M. B. Harper acreage adjacent to the Barrett Mill site.

Sellers continued his land transactions on

This is Robinson's second "strip center" in Spring; the first burned in 1917. The structure is only one example of Robinson's many building projects in the town. This historic picture merits a close examination: the post office is in the first building. The poster on the front advertising savings stamps tells us the time is World War II. The second building is a barber shop. The faint sign on the third building reveals that Mallott's Grocery is housed there. Note that ice cream is 5 cents a cone. Willard Mallott Jr. sits on a bread box on the front of the store. Ironically, this set of buildings also burned—in 1943. A restaurant located on the same spot in Old Town Spring burned in 1999!

Above: *Several of Robinson's houses are still in use as shops in Old Town Spring.*

Below: *Bright colors and decorations now ornament what were once dwellings in order to draw customers to the shops of Old Spring. Yet, the exterior style of the houses remains true to original form and reveals the early date of the cottages.*

Above: *Mr. and Mrs. Robinson remained active contributors in the community all of their days. This picture of Robert and Elizabeth Robinson was taken August 29, 1942.*

Mr. Robinson died in December 1943.

— Courtesy of John Robinson

Right: *At the corner of Keith and Main is the lovely Bradley House, one of Mr. Robinson's first houses.*

One of the first post offices in Spring was housed in J. C. Sellers' Saloon and Mercantile at the corner of Hardy and Caroline Streets. Sellers sold this general store to George Goedecke, a German baker from Galveston. The Spring post office was housed in the Sellers/Goedecke mercantile for twenty-six years.

— Courtesy of John Robinson

January 7, 1907, when he sold a parcel of land, over five acres, to the Woodmen of the World, an organization similar to the Masonic Lodge, that specialized in the sale of insurance. On this land, the Woodmen of the World completed a large hall for their meetings and for community activities.

Because of its importance to the community, the Woodmen Hall deserves a digression. In a 1988 article entitled "A Fourth of July in Spring," ninety-year-old Edward Williams recalls a yesteryear Fourth of July celebration in the "just completed new [Woodmen of the World] hall." In his lively account of a small community's Independence Day celebration in the early twentieth century, Williams details the use of the hall for a large-group dinner, a political rally, and an evening dance. In fact, dances were regular events in the Woodmen Hall during the 20s and 30s. Many a Saturday night, Ralph Hanks and his musicians used their fiddles to draw out the strains of "Ten Pretty Girls" and "Put Your Little Foot" for group performances and then broke into two-steps and waltzes for

couple dancing. Avalt Meyer recalls that sometimes "dance was mixed with mash" (homebrew liquor), often making for a quarrelsome party. Fights were not uncommon when the Woodmen Hall patrons were impassioned by the "nectar of Spring Creek."

Other lively community events occurred in the Woodmen Hall. Theatrical presentations, such as the "Womanless Wedding," directed by Natalene Sellers and starring the men of Immanuel Church, were performed there. At this particular event, Henry Roth, the largest man in the church, who lived just off Spring-Stuebner Road, portrayed the bride; and tiny Albert Paetzold, who scarcely weighed a hundred pounds, enacted the part of the groom. Absurd casting of local men and outlandish female costumes adorning rough farmers and various other macho churchmen left the community weak from laughter.

As the Depression helped make Spring a quieter town, the Works Progress Administration converted the Woodmen building into a combination basketball court/auditorium for

Taken long after the Sellers Addition was part of a teeming railroad town, these deteriorating buildings still capture the appearance of this part of Spring as it stretched along the east side of the railroad track. In the foreground is the hospital, then the Sellers' Hotel and other buildings. The photograph was taken in the late 20's after the railroad roundhouse moved from the town.

— Courtesy of John Robinson

the Spring Independent School District since the school at that time was located next to the hall. John Robinson, who played basketball in the Woodmen Hall, describes the basketball court in Kessler's *Narrative Ethnography of Spring*:

[It] was not big enough for a full size basketball court and we had eight by eight posts running up and down the baselines of the basketball court . . . We had a little barrier and right over that barrier was the orchestra pit. Then the ceiling was only about two feet above the backboard, so you learned to shoot as a bullet not as an arch shot.

The school district had that location by the Woodmen Hall, thanks to J. C. and Julia Sellers. Again, the Sellers owned the tract adjoining the Woodmen of the World property on the south side, a tract on which a school stood at the time. On December 19, 1907, Sellers conveyed 3.29 acres of that land to Trustees of the Spring Independent School District. The deed reads as follows:

KNOW ALL MEN BY THESE PRESENTS:

THAT, I, J. C. Sellers, of the County of Harris in the State aforesaid Texas for and in consideration of the sum of Ten Dollars $10.00/100 Dollars to me in hand paid by the Trustees of Spring Independent School District,

Have granted, sold, and conveyed, and by these presents do grant, sell and convey

George Goedecke and his handsome family posed for this picture in 1912. On the back row from left to right are Karl Goedecke, Sophie, George Jr., Ella, and Annie. On the front row are William (Willie), George Sr., his wife, Sophie Holzwarth Goedecke, and the youngest child, August. In 1900, just before the great storm, George Goedecke bought Sellers' store and moved his family from Galveston to Spring. Goedecke became a leader in the community and was instrumental in founding Immanuel United Church in 1916.

— Courtesy of Rudolph Goedecke

unto the said Trustees of Spring Independent School District of Harris County, Texas. Of the County of Harris in the State of Texas all that certain parcel or tract of land . . . described [below].

For more than forty years, this site, purchased (or donated) for *ten dollars* served as the location for a school in the Spring Independent School District. Thanks to Arthur Bayer for his information on these important land transactions.

Early Postal Service in Spring

Sellers was also prominent in the development of the post office in Spring. One of the first post offices was located in the corner of Sellers Mercantile Store on Hardy Street. Sellers, in 1900, sold this general store to George Goedecke, a German baker from Galveston. Goedecke proceeded to become a leader in the town, involving himself in several areas of civic development. The post office continued to operate in Goedecke's store for a time. If accurate calculations can be made from the documents related to change of venue for post offices, the Spring post office was housed in the Sellers/Goedecke mercantile for twenty-six years.

Jim Wheat, compiler of *Postmasters and Post Offices in Texas 1846-1930,* records twelve postmasters for Spring from the beginnings of a postal system in Spring to 1930. The list is as follows:

Callahan Pickette, July 7, 1873
Clegg, W. O., September 24, 1873
Sommer, Charles, December 2, 1873
Sommer, Mrs. Adele, November 9, 1876
Bender Lina, March 17, 1879
Bender, Jr., Charles, May 11, 1886
Sellers, Lula O., April 10, 1890
Sellers, Mrs. Julia, December 15, 1891
Townsend, Homer E., August 29, 1899
Sellers, John C., December 18, 1906
Pevateaux, Lafayette, September 8, 1911
(and P approved by the President and PS confirmed by the Senate for terms beginning on July 1, 1920; February 14, 1922; March 15, 1926; November 1, 1928)
(Spring Post Office was relegated or changed from Presidential Class to Fourth Class on July 1, 1928.)
Desmond, Louisa H., July 15, 1929

Records from the Post Office Department, Topographer's Office, preserve copies of questionnaires completed by postmasters. These questionnaires are/were used "to determine with as much accuracy as possible, the relative positions of Post Offices" so that they may be "corrected delineated" on the Postal Depart-

Charlie Klein in his mail delivery wagon. Mr. Klein had been postmaster of the Klein Post Office from 1902 until it closed in 1906. He became mail carrier in Spring and delivered mail for the next thirty years, never missing a day's work. He later got a motor vehicle to take him on his route.
— Courtesy Klein Archives

Records in the Post Office Depart, Topographer's Office, Washington, D.C. give information about the location of post offices in Spring and names of the postmasters. This sample report is from Julia Sellers, 1898, describing the location of the Spring post office.

Mrs. L. H. Desmond describes the location of the Spring post office in 1935. Mrs. Desmond was postmistress of the Spring post office in Robinson's strip center when it burned in 1943.

In 1902, the post office moved to H. E. Townsend's General Merchandise store on Midway Street.

— Courtesy of John Robinson

ment's maps. On record is one questionnaire, completed by Julia Sellers, August 6, 1898, postmistress at the time. She worked from the post office in the corner of Sellers Saloon and Mercantile on Hardy Street.

Another document from the Topographer's Office is a request by Homer E. Townsend, October 16, 1902, asking to move the location of the post office. Townsend notes that the number of inhabitants in the village of Spring in 1902 is two hundred and that the post office will serve that same number. A third document is a questionnaire completed by Mrs. L. H. Desmond, October 29, 1935. During her tenure, Mrs. Desmond oversaw the post office, then located in Robinson's strip center, and was postmistress there when the building burned in 1941. These forms are taken from the Post Office Department's Reports of Site Locations, 1837-1950.

Two citizens of Spring who remember early twentieth century activities recall the Spring post offices. William T. ("Uncle Willie") Wunsche was for many years Spring's beloved historian/storyteller. Willie's "first postal recollection is 'a bunch of pigeon-hole boxes' in J. C. Sellers's general store. The post office was on one end of the counter, and beer was sold from a beer box on the other end." Wunsche recalls that Homer Townsend moved the post office to a store west of Goedecke's, still in the original "Town of Spring." Later, Dr. J. C. Sellers, J. C. Sellers's son, relocated the post office to the new part of town (the "Robinson Addition") by Wunsche Bros. and next door to Sellers's drugstore. According to Wunsche, " 'Homer Townsend built a new store on Midway,' " and for a time the post office was in this store. The post office sat on a store counter, but it was " 'a little better than before. Had more boxes. There were more people in town by then,' " declares Wunsche in Polly Duke's article, "The Case of the Perplexing Post Offices." When Willie Wunsche left to serve in World War I, Lafayette [sic] Telesphore Pevateaux was postmaster at a location on Main at Preston Street.

After World War I, the postal department established a rural mail route in Spring. Wunsche had a vivid memory of that first mail route. He says:

> "When Charlie Richey started a rural mail route out of Spring, he had a little brown mare, and carried the mail in saddlebags . . . . It was always a horse route until Richey gave it up.
>
> "When Charlie Klein got the route, he used a horse for a while. Then he bought a Brush automobile from Peden Iron and Steel Company. It looked about like the jeeps you see running around here now. It was a single seat outfit with single cylinder . . . The route was 22 miles long every day . . . ."

Former resident of Spring, Edward E. Williams, also recalls mail service, again in Pevateaux' post office:

> Mr. Pevateaux was postmaster. The post office was very small. It had a few private boxes and the general delivery window where everyone got their mail. When the trains came in the postmaster went across the road (*I said road, not street*) and looked through the letters to see if there were any special delivery or letters edged in black.

According to Williams, these two types of letters were hand-delivered: Special delivery "cost ten cents more than regular letters" for the privilege of personal delivery, and letters edged in black were death notifications—their personal delivery was "a courtesy the postmaster performed." The general delivery window at the post office was tended by Pevateaux' wife. When people called for their mail, she looked through the thin stack of letters and usually said "No mail today."

Spring: The Railroad Boomtown

Uncle Willie Wunsche died in April 1985, but he leaves us with much first-hand information about turn-of-the-twentieth-century Spring. In interviews, such as the one in "As recalled by W. T. Wunsche . . . ." in the *North Harris County News,* Willie describes life in the Spring railroad town of 1900. Wunsche remembers how the railroad, which had become the International and Great Northern Railroad, ran through the town and kept the "settlement active as a farming trades area." When the Fort Worth Line of

William Wunsche, "Uncle Willie," was Spring's resident historian before his death in April 1985. Willie leaves us much information about the early days of Spring and the importance of the railroad to the town.

the Calvert, Waco, and Brazos Valley Railroad Company was laid to intersect with the I&GN shortly after the turn of the century (1901-1903), Spring became a major switchyard with a roundhouse, fourteen track yards, and almost two hundred railroad workers who were stationed in the town.

Another of the Wunsches, Willie's brother, Earl, sat for a *Houston Chronicle* interview in 1970. He, too, attests to the importance of the railroad in the development of Spring. Earl Wunsche says that at the turn of the century, "Spring was a thriving railroad center with a round-house, a depot, and three rail divisions: south to Houston and Galveston, west to Mart, and north to Palestine."

Because of railroad expansion, the town experienced a dramatic building boom. The need for hotels, rooming houses, and places of entertainment to accommodate railroad employ-ees and railroad trade brought a rash of new business structures, most of them wooden, built from area pine timber that was milled locally. Samples of these businesses included the Sellers Hotel, built in 1902; the Harvey Hotel; and the Womack Boarding House. Wunsche Bros. Saloon, which still stands at the corner of Midway and Hardy Streets, was built during this time, along with gambling houses, an opera house, Dr. Dunham's hospital, and a bank. Pictures, many of which are on display in the Spring Historical Museum, exist as records of boomtown Spring. They depict the facade of a frontier town, not unlike those shown in Hollywood's western movies.

The Spring train depot, at this point located just across the tracks from Wunsche Bros., was built of the same pine siding as the other buildings. The depot was an elegant structure with faux Victorian trim, cut from galvanized sheet

Because of railroad traffic, businesses sprang up overnight. The Sellers Hotel on the east side of the railroad tracks was built in 1902.
— Courtesy of John Robinson

Below: *A Harvey Hotel, one in the Harvey chain of hotels, located in Spring. The Harvey "girls," dancers and entertainers, were famous throughout the West in their own right. Did Harvey girls dance in Spring? Seemingly so.*
— Courtesy of John Robinson

Above: *When the Fort Worth Line of the Calvert, Waco, and Brazos Valley Railroad Company was laid to intersect with the International and Great Northern rail line, Spring became a major switchyard. Here is the Spring roundhouse in 1902.*

— Courtesy of John Robinson

Below: *The illustration reveals the workings of a railroad roundhouse such as the one in Spring. The establishment of a roundhouse in Spring made the town a hub of railroad activity. (Thanks to Ernest Mignon Medlin for this document.)*

Why a "Round House"?

Railroad steam engines had predetermined routes. For example: Spring to Houston and back. But the freight cars might be headed for Galveston or Beaumont. When a train came into a yard, the engine was separated for necessary maintenance before being "turned around" to return from whence it came. Cars from all incoming trains would be moved onto various designated tracts and attached to a serviced steam engine heading toward the freight cars' final destination.

1. Turn table
2. Service bay for minor repairs
3. Washroom and welding shop
4. Spare materials
5. Machine shop
6. Back shop for major repairs
7a. Sand pipe
7b. Water spout
8. Sand pile
9. Coal chute
10. Jumbo track (wrecker train)
11. Water spout
12. Inspection pit, inspection office and water lab
13. Blow down track
14. Fire knockers pit
15. Fire knockers pit
16. Wash track
17. Clerk's office and train crew waiting room
18. Power plant
19. Storage track (parked extra locomotives)
20. Ash pit clamshell (big crane)
21. Track to power plant
22. Outbound service track
23. Outbound service track
24. Engine parking track
25. Ramp for coal cars to be used in coal chute

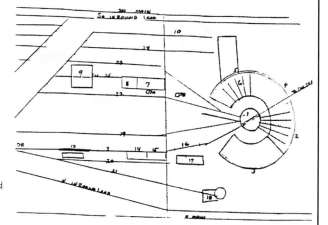

Service Track—First, the water in the boiler is tested to determine number of times the boiler needs be "blown" for cleaning; the boiler is then flushed with clean water accordingly. Then the boiler is inspected.

Fire Knockers—After the boiler is cleaned, fire knockers put the engine over another pit where extra ashes and clinkers are removed from the fire box.

Wash Track—The engine is hosed down with soapy water and the windows are washed.

Hostler—A person who puts the engine on the Turn Table. The entine is greased with allomite every time it comes into the yard. Once a month the boiler and pipes are totally cleaned in the back shop. The engine is then turned around, filled with water, dry sand (for traction) and coal.

Flags and Lanterns—Signal flags on the engine when one train had two sections: white flag is on the first section and green is on the second. The lanterns were changed in agreement with the flags, with red reserved for the end.

Left: *Pictured is Goedecke's delivery wagon. George Goedecke, who took over a saloon and mercantile in 1899, offered a delivery service for the growing population of Spring.*

Below: *The shop of the blacksmith/wheelwright was a popular spot.*

— Photos courtesy of John Robinson

metal. At the busy station, trains stopped daily, bringing passengers and goods to Spring, and taking passengers and goods from Spring to Houston or to points north. As a result of this boom, by 1910 twelve hundred people walked the streets of old Spring.

Those twelve hundred *did not always walk*, however. Traffic which came in by rail, plus the lack of automobiles, motivated a need for a taxi service in Spring. John Brady hired Phelmo Burke, a very young Willie Wunsche, and an even younger Earl Wunsche to operate a jitney business out of the Cline-Harper House (now known as Whitehall on Main Street). For a few cents, one could get a ride to Westfield, Humble, Aldine, or any other spot within a radius of twenty or twenty five miles of downtown Spring!

Right: *By 1910, the census recorded twelve hundred people in Spring, Texas, railroad boom town. The depot sat in the heart of the town, its pulsing traffic nourishing the boom around it. The building was an elegant structure with faux Victorian trim cut from galvanized sheet metal.*

— Courtesy of John Robinson

Below: *Astride his horse, his wife on the porch of their family store, O. E. Robertson poses on Midway Street, against the hastily assembled, boomtown of Spring. The two-story building in the far background is Wunsche Bros. The picture dates from 1910, shortly after the Robertsons were married. Later the Robertson family moved to Dodge, Texas. O. E. Robertson died in Oil City, Louisiana, on December 15, 1940. His devoted wife, devastated at the loss of her husband, died just a few days later and was buried on Christmas Eve.*

— Courtesy of Clay Mills

As with people today, the people of Spring were fascinated by the great steam engines that ran through the town. In this 1921 photograph, a steam engine has derailed somewhere along the Hardy Street track. Spectators have gathered to witness the scene. Men in suits and hats stand around, causing one to think that this event may be filling a Sunday afternoon. Notice that one gentleman has brought his baby to see the big train up close. Workers are pondering a solution to the problem, but the spectators just seem to be enjoying the excitement!

— Courtesy of Diana Haude

At first glance, this 1933 picture of three-year old Billy Powell seems just a camera shot of a cute baby, posed on a box-car rung by his grandfather. But the picture is more than a family remembrance of a child. The picture evokes a town memory of the Spring water tower. Behind Billy stands the railroad water tower, an 85,000 gallon tank with an open top, used to fill the tenders of great steam engines that roared into Spring. Located just over the tracks on East Hardy at Noble Street, the tank furnished water for two drop spouts—the one in the picture, which serviced trains on the main line to Palestine and another one on the line across Hardy Street that provided water for trains of the Ft. Worth/Waco division.

The tower represents a colorful part of Spring history. At the turn of the twentieth century, Spring was the railroad's watering hole, both for cattle being shipped West by rail and for the steam engines. The railroad pumped water up from Spring Creek, using a gasoline pump. The water was put into a holding tank and then directed into vats for cows that were unloaded from the trains. In Spring, these animals were fed and watered and then reloaded in their cattle cars to continue the journey to Texas towns such as San Angelo and Abilene. The creek water was also pumped into the water tower. Part of the four-inch pipe line that carried the water from Spring Creek may still be found in the ground today.

Buster Bayer, son of sawmill magnate Gus Bayer, can remember recreational uses of the water tank. In the 1930s, Buster and his friends went skinny dipping in the tank during Spring's hot summer nights. Buster says that Spring folks also crawled up the tank ladder and fished in the open top of the tower, catching trout and small catfish brought up from the creek.

Later, an artesian well, drilled across the street, provided water for the tank and for the town water system.

The exact date of the construction of the water tower is unknown, but it certainly served its purpose when Spring was a railroad hub. The water tank has been gone a long time now, torn down when train engines no longer depended on water for steam, but lore about the tank continues to amuse older Spring citizens.

Growth of the Lumber Industry

The densely wooded land of the area and the need for lumber spawned sawmill after sawmill. The first sawmill in Spring was on Spring School Road; the kiln for that mill was later converted into the Spring opera house. John Robinson offers names of some of the early mills: the Barrett Saw Mill; the Burke Lumber Yard; the Cline Lumber Yard; and the Harless Tie Mill. The Bender Lumber Company, which became one of the largest and most lucrative mills in Harris County, began in the woods on Riley-Fuzzel Road, and a tram brought Bender's lumber to the railroad. In about 1886, the Bender Mill moved to Humble.

Bayer Lumber Co., Spring's most important sawmill, came later. In 1927, Gus Bayer opened Bayer's Excelsior Mill, a mill that produced packing material from wood and palmetto leaves, inside the triangle of the railroad tracks. Then, Bayer built a sawmill by the Excelsior Mill and later erected a larger mill on Aldine-Westfield Road. Bayer Lumber Co. contributed to the life of the town even after the boom days were gone. Mr. Bayer and his sons carried on a

---

Spring, Texas, _____ 1914

M _____ May 2

BOUGHT OF **GEO. GOEDECKE**

DEALER IN

GENERAL MERCHANDISE

CREDITOR

By	doz. Eggs @		
By	lbs. Butter @		

DEBTOR

Coffee ✓		50
Meal ✓		85
Flour ✓	1	50
Sugar ✓		50
Soap ✓		15
Soda ✓		05
B m Tob ✓		10
Tob ✓		10
Thread ✓		05
Snuff ✓		25
Leve ✓		15
Beans ✓		40
Coffee ✓		40
		5 00

This 1914 receipt for "general merchandise" purchased from George Goedecke's store vividly demonstrates the change in cost of goods over the last 100 years and the dramatic change in bookkeeping! Date: May 2, 1914.
—Courtesy of Gertie Mae Salyers

There were specialty shops in Spring even in 1910! Here Grace West poses in her mother's millinery shop.

— Courtesy of John Robinson

Timber was plentiful in the Spring area. In fact, for many the trees were a bother—and a challenge. Land had to be cleared for farming, for pastureland for cattle, and for roads. These workers are at the task of felling great pines to free the land for other uses. No wonder with so much timber that sawmills located in Spring and in the surrounding areas.
— Courtesy of Diana Haude

With the building boom in Spring, lumber was in great demand. Spring spawned sawmills, and in turn sawmills spawned Spring! Here is a picture of Bush Bros. Mill, one of the first mills in Spring.

— Courtesy of John Robinson

family business at the sawmill site until May of 1954 when most of the mill burned.

John Robinson recalls working in the Bay and Barren Veneer Mill in old Spring, located on the east side of the railroad track. Robinson tells of his wages and his job:

We got paid seventeen cents an hour, a dollar and seventy-seven cents for ten hours.

They would cut trees and then steam them and then roll them out [with a machine]. Employees just pulled those thin sheets maybe forty or fifty feet down a platform. Then they'd clip the sheets off. And then we'd go and get another sheet. It would go through a machine that would cut it at certain widths. And we would take those pieces and stack them so they could dry out.

Above: *In 1927, Gus Bayer opened Bayer's Excelsior Mill, pictured here. Because of the mill's proximity to the railroad track, the ice storage box, shown in the middle of the photograph, was located by the mill. The ice storage box, 8 feet by 8 feet, was used by the railroad as just that—an ice storage room. The ice held in this insulated container was brought in to use in cooling refrigerator cars. These refrigerator cars were the vehicles for shipping produce such as sweet potatoes, Irish potatoes, and cabbage from Spring to St. Louis and on to New York. R. L. Robinson, Spring developer, who was the railroad agent in Spring at the time, was the first in Spring to ship his farm crops in this way.*

Right: *The most remarkable of Spring's mills was Bayer Lumber Company. Beginning in 1927, Gus Bayer, Jr. became the "lumber tycoon" of Spring. This delightful portrait is of a young Bayer and his family. Gustave (Gus) Bayer Jr. is on the left; then his brother Frank; his father, Gustave Sr.; and mother Bertha Laut Bayer.*
— Courtesy of the
Bayer Archives

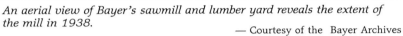

An aerial view of Bayer's sawmill and lumber yard reveals the extent of the mill in 1938.

— Courtesy of the Bayer Archives

Arthur Bayer, Gus Bayer's son, continues to use the old sawmill office as his point of operation for various ventures in Spring. Arthur graciously shares his memories and historical memorabilia with the community. The sign Arthur stands by depicts the original telephone prefix for the area, SKyline!

Violence in Spring

The population in Spring in the early part of the twentieth century was definitely volatile—composed of lusty railroad hands (many of them hot-tempered Irishmen), strong-willed Germans, and tough sawmill workers! Such a group was not easy to control, and quarrels were frequent and could be deadly. Avalt Meyer, whose father farmed down Aldine-Westfield Road, recalls stories of shootings from the upper verandah of Wunsche Bros. Saloon. Avalt's cousin, Paul Schultz, was a victim of Spring's violence: Schultz was shot and killed on Spring Station Road (now Spring-Cypress) by someone who had a grudge against him. Theresa McGinley in her book *Just a Whistle Stop Away, the History of Old Town Spring*, quotes Joe Monroe, a retired railroad worker: " 'It was wild. . . . Women would walk a block out of their way to get by [Wunsche Bros.] because there were so many fights going on . . . I fought four farmers once who took up for the Kaiser in 1917.' "

A SHREWISH DAME

Not all Spring ladies were genteel and avoided violence; some enjoyed tempestuous encounters. Mrs. Annie Hoffmann, daughter of George Goedecke, recalls the antics of a quarrelsome woman who was in truth Spring's scourge. In the early years of the twentieth century, this shrewish dame rode her horse around Spring and dominated her "lessors" with a whip—which she wielded generously. Once, the woman became angry at a male servant of hers for wearing her husband's clothes, clothes she had given to the servant. She forced the man to disrobe and to run before her whip down the railroad tracks from Spring to Westfield, a distance of four miles. Another time, the same lady stormed the schoolhouse, ready to whip the teacher for some infraction against a child who was a ward of the woman. One source commented on this legendary Spring native, declaring that the woman carried a jug of home-brew with her, slung over the saddle horn, and took an occasional swig whenever she needed a shot of fresh vigor. Ever on the defensive, this vicious horsewoman caused many to quail before her wrath!

THE SHOOTING OF CLINT HARLESS

Spring's most famous story of violence and lawlessness centers around another who primarily used a horse for his means of mobility,

Constable W. Clint Harless. Harliss, remembered for his efforts to keep order in old Spring, is alternately called "Constable" and "Sheriff" because he was both. He became a Deputy Sheriff under Harris County Sheriff Frank Hammond and served as resident Constable in Spring as well. Born November 23, 1891, Sheriff Harless was just twenty-four years old in 1915, a big man who sat tall in the saddle as he rode horseback around Spring. Some have called Harless indolent; other remember him as formidable. In any case, his height and breadth of girth commanded respect of all who even remotely thought of taking the law in their own hands.

Harless came to his tragic end upholding the law. On Wednesday night, April 14, 1915, Clint Harless was shot as he sought to apprehend a man, Louis Utley, who had been charged with burglary in Montgomery County and who had sought asylum in the home of a relative at Spring . In his confession, Utley said he shot out of fear: "That officer looked like a giant to me. . . . He came riding up on his horse [and yelled at me to] 'come out'. . . . It was kill or be killed." Grabbing a loaded Winchester, Utley pointed the rifle at Harless who, too late, tried to duck. The bullet hit Harless in the neck, and he fell from his horse, alive but mortally wounded.

Witnesses remembered well the sound of the rifle: Adelle Robinson was milking a cow when she heard the shot. Paul Klein in his home nearby heard the gun fire and ran to the scene. From all corners, spectators converged on the place where the high sheriff had fallen.

Just as the town *looked* like a set in a Western movie, the news articles about this event in Spring's history *read* like a script for a Western movie. Harless, alert and aware of what was happening to him, was placed on an International and Great Northern train and rushed to Houston where Westheimer's ambulance met the train and took him to the Baptist

Spring. Looking east down Midway toward the train station. Spring had the look of a Western frontier town. Just as frontier towns had their share of violence, so did Spring!

— Courtesy of John Robinson

Above: Work *was hard—life was hard in "frontier" Spring. Can we not imagine that when this group of workers left the job and "let their hair down" they could be reckless in their merriment! "Hard work, hard play" might have been the motto of the town.*

Below: *These cowboys, Riley Fussel, Ernest Hillegeist, Adolph Bender, and Allie Bender, reinforce the idea that Spring was much like a western cowtown. The horse was important for transportation and for rounding up cattle, especially in Spring Creek bottom land. A mix of railroad men, sawmill workers, and cowboys made for a volatile population in Spring.*

— Photos courtesy of John Robinson

This grouping gives insight into life in early Spring. As noted in other scenes, the mode of travel for work and pleasure was the horse. Here, the rider's rifle is cradled across his lap. Wide-brimmed, large-crowned hats top the costume of each man, although the younger men have removed their hats (in respect to the photographer or to honor the formality of the occasion) while their elders wear their hats. The man on the horse, and more clearly, the man sitting with the women, have handlebar mustaches. Everyone is nicely dressed: the older woman has a light colored blouse and dark skirt; the girls have light dresses with ribbon sashes, suggesting Sunday and church, or preparations for a party. For a backdrop, the photographer has selected the farm home, fences, and barns.

— Courtesy of John Robinson

Sanitarium. The April 15, 1915, *Houston Chronicle* reports:

> The wounded man, conscious and courageous, was taken uptown Thursday morning for an X-ray examination. It was found that the bullet had entered his neck on the left side and, after shattering the vertebra, had lodged in the right side. It has not been removed for the patient is not able to undergo an operation.
>
> "Inasmuch as a spinal cord has been broken, we fear there is no chance of recovery," said an attending physician.

To add to the dramatics of the tragic story, one account of Utley's escape is that he left Spring on the very same train that carried his victim to get medical assistance. In Houston, Special Officer O. B. Bobo had received a description of Utley a few minutes before the train arrived. According to Mr. Bobo, a man who resembled Utley leaped off the blind side of the train, and Bobo took two shots at him. A hunt ensued, but the escapee was nowhere to be found. Utley's own story did not coincide: Utley said he ran away from Spring after the shooting,

following the woods to Conroe. He spent the night in a railroad tank near Shepherd, Texas. Before the accused criminal was apprehended, a one hundred dollar reward had been offered for him and posses with bloodhounds had scoured the bottom land around Spring Creek searching for him.

Clint Harless "steadily grew weaker" and died Thursday, April 15, 1915. The *Houston Chronicle* validates the size of the young law officer: "Harless, though only 24 years old, [was] 6 feet 6 inches tall and [weighed] 350 pounds. Because of his size, the circumstances of Harless's preparation for burial were also unusual. A *Post* news article gives this detail:

> Constable Harless was the biggest peace officer in the State, and no casket big enough for his body could be found in Houston. Therefore, the Sid Westheimer Undertaking Company, who took the body in charge, had a casket made to order.

Clint Harless was "one of the best liked officers in the County." A retinue of lawmen from all over the area witnessed his funeral, held at

Clint Harless is buried in Budde Cemetery in the family plot beside his father. The dates of his birth and death are incorrect—by one year.

2 o'clock Sunday, April 18, from his residence in Spring. Harless was not married; his survivors were his parents, Mr. and Mrs. F. G. Harless, three brothers, and two sisters.

In Budde Cemetery, in the Harless family plot, one gravestone reads: "Brother W. G. Harless b. Oct. 24, 1890 d. Apr. 15, 1914." Even though the initials are W. G. and the dates on the stone do not match Harless's birth and death by one year, one must assume that this twenty-four year old who rests beside F. G. Harless (1846-1919) is Spring's own lawman, killed doing his duty.

Clint Harless has not gone unrecognized: A

Constable W. Clint Harless, shot and killed in the line of duty, is pictured here on a Spring street. The intricacies of the story of Harless' demise rival fiction in terms of drama and sensation! Harless is the man on the far right.
— Courtesy of John Robinson

FRIDAY, APRIL 16, 1915
HOUSTON DAILY POST

Second floor, 719 Main Street, Zoe Theatre Entrance (Take Elevator)

CONSTABLE HARLESS DEAD FROM WOUND

Was Shot by Negro in Spring Wednesday Night.

It Is Thought Man Wanted by Officers Came to Houston and Was Fired At—$100 Reward Offered.

Constable W. Clint Harless, who was shot at Spring Wednesday evening by a negro for whom he held a warrant, died Thursday afternoon at 2:45 o'clock. The bullet that struck him entered his neck and ranged downward, shattering the spinal column.

That the negro who shot Constable Harless came to Houston on the same train that brought the wounded officer, and was shot at as he got off at the International and Great Northern station, is the belief of Special Officer O. D. Bobo.

According to Mr. Bobo, the negro who got off the train on the blind side fitted exactly the description of the negro who shot Mr. Harless. The special officer had received a description of the negro a few minutes before the train arrived with instructions to be on the lookout for him.

FIRED TO SHOTS AT FLEEING NEGRO.

The negro jumped off the train and ran between two cars, coming in eight feet of him, said Mr. Bobo, and as he did so the officer fired two shots at him. It is believed that neither of the shots took effect. The matter was reported to police officers and a hunt was made for the negro Wednesday night, but he was not found.

A negro at Spring reported that he met a negro about three miles north of Spring a short time after the shooting. The negro told him, he said, that he had killed a white man and was Louisiana bound. It is thought possible that the negro got on the International and Great Northern passenger train bearing Mr. Harless at Westgate, which was the only stop that the train made before reaching Houston.

SHERIFF HAS OFFERED REWARD OF $100

Sheriff Hammond has offered a reward of $100 for the arrest and conviction of the slayer of Constable Harless, who was one of the best liked officers in the county. All night Wednesday and all day Thursday officers and citizens scoured

the country around Spring, looking for the negro.

Bloodhounds from county convict camp No. 2 were put on the trail and followed the negro to where the International and Great Northern crosses the old tram track. From there the trail led to Spring creek, but the creek was so swollen that he turned northwest toward Conroe. Then the dogs lost the trail, which had grown cold. Every town in that section of the country has been notified and a lookout is being maintained at each place for the negro.

After being taken to the hospital Constable Harless steadily grew weaker, and although he possessed enough strength to undergo an X-ray examination with out losing consciousness, his strength gradually failed him. His death was not unexpected for the physicians, after seeing, by means of the X-ray, what the bullet had done, said that he could not survive.

BIGGEST PEACE OFFICER IN THE STATE

Over six feet and six inches in height, Constable Harless was the biggest peace officer in the State, and no casket big enough for his body could be found in Houston. Therefore the Sid Westheimer Undertaking company, who took the body in charge, had a casket made to order.

Constable Harless was shot Wednesday evening about 6.30 o'clock as he rode up to a negro's house on the outskirts of the negro settlement at Spring. The negro who shot him saw him coming and going into the house grabbed a rifle and fired through a window.

He is survived by his father and mother, Mr. and Mrs. F. G. Harless of Austin, three brothers John and Lee Harless of Spring and Joe Harless of Austin, and two sisters, Mrs. Mary E. Stephenson of Houston and Miss Laura Harless of Lagrange.

The remains will be shipped to Spring Friday morning at 7 o'clock by the Sid Westheimer Undertaking company and the funeral will be held at Spring.

Constable W. Clint Harless

This article, among many, gives the lurid details of the shooting of the young law officer.

banner in his honor has been placed on the Harris County Sheriffs' Department flag, and his name is inscribed on the Texas Peace Officers' Memorial in Austin and on the National Memorial in Washington D. C.

A concluding note: Harliss's murder suspect, trying to escape under an alias, was finally apprehended in Livingston, Texas, seemingly as frightened as he had been when he fired the Winchester. Utley was a small man—described as "under medium size"—and weighed less than 120 pounds. He had a missing front tooth and "a decided speech impediment." How has Hollywood managed to miss this true story of unique characters, of violence, of fear, of mishap and layers of irony?

TWO WHO WERE IN THE WRONG PLACE AT THE WRONG TIME

August Wunsche tells a story of tragedy in his own family, brought on by an unexplainable act of violence.

Since his birth on July 17, 1912, August has lived his life within two miles of Spring proper, except for brief periods including three years in the Army Air Force (1941-1945), during which time he served in the Middle East, Africa, and Italy. Wunsche was discharged as a sergeant with the Victory Medal, the Sharp Shooter's Medal, and the Good Conduct Medal to his credit.

August Wunsche says that in May of 1929, his sister Olena, twenty years old at the time, worked during the week for a Houston family as a cook. On Fridays, her boyfriend, Edward Stone, went to Houston on Highway 19 to get Olena and bring her home for a couple of free days. On the weekend of this story, the young couple had a Saturday night date; they spent the evening at Woodmen Hall where Olena danced every dance. She loved to dance; Edward did not. He just enjoyed watching everyone else.

The next day, Sunday, Edward Stone picked up Olena at the Wunsche home to take her back to her job in Houston. That was the last time the Wunsche family was to see either of them alive. Early Monday morning, Edward's body was found beside his car in a solitary Lover's Lane near Aldine. He had been shot. Olena was

nowhere around. Later in the day, Dick Hartmann, a Spring man who worked for Harris County, found her on Aldine-Westfield Road. She, too, had been shot—in the back: from all appearances she had jumped from a moving car and had run, only to be gunned down.

Investigation into the murders of Olena Wunsche and Edward Stone brought more mystery to an already unexplainable crime. The couple had been last seen in a little bar near Aldine where they had stopped to get a drink. Seemingly, they had traveled on, had decided to park in an isolated area, and had been overpowered by their attackers—Edward killed on the spot—Olena transported away only to be murdered later. Stories that circulated about the crime ranged from gossip about the motive to rumors that the get-away car the murderers used was hidden in someone's barn. All stories seem to have been just speculation.

The deaths of Olena Wunsche and Edward Stone shocked the Spring community, and that grief and concern, at least in one instance, may have been exploited, according to Awalt Meyer. When election time came around, one candidate for sheriff broke the news that he "had someone in jail and had solved the murders of the Wunsche girl and the Stone boy." After the candidate was elected, the prisoner, an unlikely suspect in the first place, was released. The murders of two young people who seemingly were in the wrong place at the wrong time remain unsolved.

Spring State Bank, Bank Robbers, and the Heroics of H. D. Brown

The little bank of Spring witnessed its share of excitement and violence in those reckless days. According to John Robinson, "'On May 16, 1910, the state granted a charter to Spring State Bank, with a capital of $10,000.00 and 100 shares of stock.'" Initial directors of the bank were J. C. Sellers, R. L. Robinson, George Goedecke, C. M. Britain, H. E. Townsend, C. F. Wunsche, and A. Bender. The first frame bank building burned in the devastating fire of 1917, and the bank was rebuilt and relocated on Gentry Street. The new building, one of only three brick structures in the Spring area, was constructed, according to the owner (as the story goes), so that the bank would never again burn! True to the reputed plan, this second bank remains intact today with the original vault available for viewing.

The bank building never burned again, but other types of volatile times—and tragic times— were to come for Spring State Bank: on July 5, 1925, C. Sibley, cashier at the bank, drowned in Spring Creek; his successor was Homer D. Brown, then bookkeeper for Klein Grocery Store. Reports of Mr. Brown's bold actions teach us all that one should never underestimate the courage of a bookkeeper.

Around noon on May 24, 1932, two men drove up in front of Spring State Bank and stopped their car. After looking up and down Midway Street, the pair entered the bank. The former teller's daughter, Mavis Sibley, a sixteen-year-old high school student who had just started working in the bank, leaves an eyewitness account. In her story, the men audaciously ordered Brown and Sibley to raise their hands above their heads. Nervously brandishing a sawed-off shot gun, one bandit told Sibley: "Just sit still little lady and you won't be hurt." By the time the robbers had gathered money from the bank vault and gold coins from the cashier's counter, they had rounded up what was then a formidable sum: $7,380. Clutching their loot, the perpetrators ran out the bank door and leaped into their parked sedan. Mr. Brown seized a pistol (that had been partially visible to the robbers), ran to the door, and opened fire on the departing car! At Brown's third shot, the driver supposedly threw up his hands and fell forward on the steering wheel. According to accounts, the speed of the car slowed for a moment; then the bandit straightened up and continued to drive.

At this point, the details of this robbery get muddled. In one account, a farmer reported that after about a mile down the road, he saw the car stop and the driver change seats with the other bandit. Wounded? In the interim, Mavis Sibley, still in the bank, made a quick call to Wunsche Motor Company, located on the corner of Spring-Cypress Road and the Houston highway, in an effort to get road block in place. But the bandits had too much of a start, and there was no time to hinder their escape efforts.

Wooden facade of first Spring State Bank building.
— Courtesy of John Robinson

The next report about the robbers is that they drove about two miles west on Spring-Cypress Road, pulled into a wooded area, abandoned their car, got into an automobile with two women, and disappeared. No identification or arrests were made by public officials.

Since the bank robbery occurred during the reign of famous criminals such as John Dillinger and Bonnie Parker and Clyde Barrow, speculation ran high as to the identity of the bandits. Certain eyewitnesses were ready to testify that the robbers—at least one of the men and one of the women—were that infamous pair, Bonnie and Clyde. One gentlemen said on the day of the robbery he helped a man and woman, who looked like Bonnie and Clyde, by freeing their mired automobile from a sandbar near Spring Creek. For his assistance, the helper received a tip of $5.00 from the couple, a generous amount for the times. A lady said she directed a couple who looked just like Bonnie and Clyde to the main thoroughfare when they became lost on a dead-end road and asked for directions to the main highway. Both of these eyewitnesses claimed that Parker and Barrow, like true folk heroes, were "real nice people." The stories may

During the Depression, robberies of small-town banks were all too common. For a second time, Spring State Bank did not escape the crime wave: the bank was "held up" another time on Friday, January 6, 1933. On this occasion bankteller H. D. Brown, who again used a firearm, was able to thwart the would-be robbers. When two men entered the bank, drew pistols, and demanded money, Brown ducked under the counter and grabbed a .38 caliber pistol to defend the bank. Once more, news articles of the day show us that truth can certainly be more exciting than fiction. The *Houston Chronicle* tells the story:

> Robbery of the Spring State Bank at Spring was frustrated Friday morning when H. D. Brown, the cashier, engaged in a gun battle with two bandits who opened fire when Mr. Brown dropped behind a counter to get his own pistol instead of obeying a command to hold up his hands. The bank cashier said that a successful holdup at the bank would have involved the loss of approximately $3000.
>
> More than a dozen shots were exchanged in the fight which ensued when Brown opened fire on the hijackers with his own gun. Brown emptied the pistol at the intruders who fired eight or nine shots in return.

On May 10, 1910 the state of Texas granted a charter to this bank. The first frame bank burned; the bank was rebuilt—of brick—on Midway Street.

— Courtesy of John Robinson

be products of local fantasies, but they make nice telling all the same. Thanks to John Robinson, who generously shared his research on this exciting event in Spring's checkered history.

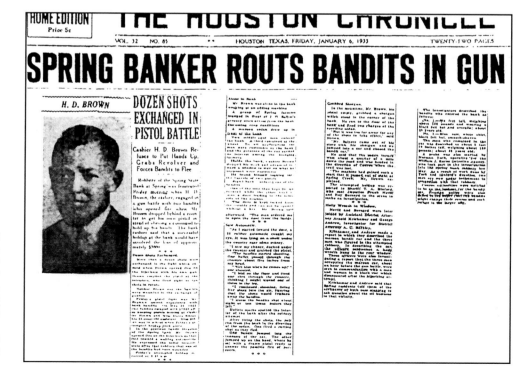

An account of bank teller H. D. Brown's heroics in the January 6, 1933, robbery of Spring State Bank. The print of the article is barely discernible, yet when deciphered, the account makes delightful reading!

— Courtesy of Brown
Family Archives

OFFICE OF
T. A. BINFORD, SHERIFF
HARRIS COUNTY

OFFICE DEPUTIES:
J. O. FLEMING, CHIEF
W. T. GLOVER, Asst.
EUGENE SANFORD, Asst.
MRS. ADICE C. SMITH, As

HOUSTON, TEXAS,
Jan. 7th., 1933.

Mr. H. D. Brown, Cashier,
Spring State Bank,
Spring, Texas.

Dear Mr. Brown:

Congratulations are due you and I want to be one of the first to offer them and am hereby extending to you mine.

To the best of my knowledge you are the first and only one that frustrated hi-jackers in an attempted bank robbery and it is a pity that we do not have more good citizens like you in cases of this kind. The only thing that I regret is that you did not wound about 3 of those would be robbers, so that some old officer could come along and pick them up afterward.

I am extending you an offer and would be more than pleased to see you accept same. I am offering you a special deputy Sheriff's commission at $1.00 per year and this special commission would give you the same authority as regular deputy.

Again extending my congratulations and stating that I would like to see you come in and accept this special commission and with my kindest personal regards, I am,

Sincerely yours,

T. A. Binford

SHERIFF HARRIS COUNTY TEXAS.

TAB/wtg

T. A. Binford, Sheriff of Harris County, honored Mr. Brown for his efforts to thwart the bank robbers!

— Brown Family Archives

dit car." Unfortunately, or perhaps fortunately, the robbers had too great a lead, and by the time Brown and Salyers reached Spring Creek, the maroon car was out of sight.

Nevertheless, H. D. Brown had established himself as a "more than your ordinary" bank teller. T. A. Binford, Sheriff of Harris County, wrote to Mr. Brown:

To the best of my knowledge you are the first and only one that frustrated hi-jackers in an attempted bank robbery and it is a pity that we do not have more good citizens like you in cases of this kind . . . .

I am offering you a special deputy Sheriff's commission at $1.00 per year and this special commission would give you the same authority as a regular deputy.

The bank did not remain in Spring long enough for Brown to use his deputy sheriff's commission. Harried by the Great Depression and weakened by the diminishing population of Spring, Spring State Bank merged with Guaranty Bond State Bank in Tomball in 1934. In a brief time, the bank moved to Tomball, but today bullet holes on the front of the little bank building testify to Spring's early shootout!

After chasing the criminals away with his pistol, Brown grabbed a shotgun and fired at them as they escaped in their maroon sedan. The *Chronicle* continues:

Bullet marks spotted the interior of the bank after the robbery attempt.

After firing the shots, the pair ran from the bank in the direction of [their] sedan. One fired a parting shot as they fled.

One bandit jumped into the . . . car. The other jumped up on the hood ready to answer the possible fire of pursuers.

Plucky Mr. Brown continued the pursuit, garnering support as he did. Brown says, "Mr. Salyers came out of his store with his shotgun and we jumped into a car and chased the ban-

Courtrooms, Jails, and Justices

If a town has lawbreakers, the town must have places to arraign them, to try them, and to confine them. Spring's first jail was located behind Robinson's strip center, and it, like many of the other buildings in that area, burned in the 1917 fire. Another of Spring's first court rooms and jails was located at the Preston Street railroad crossing. The building was a two-cell jail house "with a front room . . . . about twenty by twenty." John Robinson and his former classmate Arthur Bayer remember attending a trial in that building as part of a school project. The trial was a rape case. Robinson, with a grin, says, "We learned something about the birds and the bees there in that trial!"

Gertie Salyers says that the only time she was ever in jail was in this old court house: here is her story. Once she and a group of gentlemen were counting votes at the court house, after an election. Suddenly, they heard the report of a gun, and the air came alive with bullets whizzing through the open windows. The vote-counters scattered in all directions; Gertie says she wound up huddled in fear at the back of one of the prison cells in the court-house—as she says "in jail"! Who fired the shots? Mr. J. W. Melvin—a gentleman who had

As He Stops For 2d Haul

Ex-Convict Arrested 6 Hours After Holdup

(Continued From Page One)

by the arrival of Sheriff Kern, Assistant Chief Loyd Frazier, Night Capt. J. D. Walters and a group of deputies.

"About 1:30 we got a call relayed by radio from Julius Kuehn, the night watchman at Tomball," Sheriff Kern said.

"He told of having surprised a man burglarizing the Wilson Grocery Store in Tomball.

Description Checks

"The description of the burglar corresponded with that of the holdup gunman — young, tall, blond, wearing glasses—except that he was wearing blue work clothes instead of brown coveralls."

Mr. Kuehn said he had checked the store during his regular rounds and noticed the door open and a car parked in the back.

When he drove up, a man ran, circled around through a field, and came back.

Mr. Kuehn thought the man aimed a gun at him when he turned a light on him as he returned.

Sheriff Finds Pistol

Webb later told the sheriff it was a tire iron. He said he lost his pistol jumping a ditch in the field. The sheriff later found the pistol, a .22 revolver, beside the ditch.

"He yelled to me to get away, and I said, 'Don't shoot, I have my family with me,'" Mr. Kuehn said.

His wife and teen-age daughter had been making his rounds with him, he said.

Mr. Kuehn left, but noted the license number.

Checks With Shop

Sheriff Kern checked it through the State Department of Public Safety in Austin and found it was registered to a Harry Webb with a rural address on the East Houston road.

The sheriff, Capt. Walters, and Lt. Bill Isbell learned at that address that Webb didn't live there, but that he worked at a machine shop in the Harrisburg area.

They got the personnel manager of the shop out of bed and got still another rural address for Webb plus a phone number.

The trail finally led to 5710 Canal, where they found Webb.

Cash Found in Drawer

The sheriff discovered a big bundle of currency from the holdup in a dresser drawer.

Then Webb showed the sheriff a box with the money bags, the brown coveralls, and some of the loot from the Tomball grocery under the back steps.

He said he did a quantity of cigarets in the woods near 18th street off Hempstead Road.

Juke Box Looted

He got only about $60 cash from a juke box plus some cigarets and other small items at the grocery.

The cigarets, the car, and the pistol were all recovered. Webb said he took two buses home.

Webb was charged with robbery

WILLARD E. MALLOTT   **SHERIFF C. V. (BUSTER) KERN**

HAPPY SMILES—THE MONEY BAGS ARE RECOVERED!

The grocery loot was in a dresser drawer.

$2266 Holdup Gunman Tagged When He Makes Second Haul

By MARGARET DAVIS
Press Staff Writer

The mechanic shot a woman in the foot in a $2266 robbery at Spring.

If he hadn't gone on to burglarize a Tomball grocery for cigarets and peanuts, he might have gotten away with it.

But an alert night watchman in Tomball spotted the license number of the burglar's 1951 Mercury when he was surprised at the grocery.

Arrested in 6 Hours

Sheriff Kern traced the number through half a dozen near dead-end clues to a house on Canal street.

Six hours after the holdup at Spring, Harry Webb Jr., 28-year-old ex-convict from Illinois, was under arrest and telling the sheriff all about it.

The sheriff had recovered $864.95 of the $1272.74 cash taken in the robbery, plus the $993.36 in checks taken.

Still unaccounted for was $407.79 cash.

Webb skipped that little item in his written statement.

Parked Near Grocery

In Heights Hospital with a bullet wound through her right foot is Mrs. Dorothy Mallott, 51, wife of Willard E. Mallott, also 51, who operates Mallott's IGA Grocery and Mallott's Hardware and Variety Store in Spring.

The Mercury was parked near the grocery when Mrs. Mallott picked her husband up about 10:30 Saturday night, Mr. Mallott told Sheriff Kern.

Followed to Home

Mr. Mallott had walked out carrying two money bags, the one from the grocery store with $2064.89 in cash and checks and one from the hardware store with $201.21.

"We noticed this car right behind us as we drove toward our home ... a half-mile 'oward Highway

JULIUS F. KUEHN
Got license number

and said, 'Give me your money.'"

Mr. Mallott said he first handed his wallet to a tall, blond young man wearing glasses and dressed in brown coveralls.

Demands Money Sacks

The holdup man demanded the money sacks, too, and Mrs. Mallott got out of the car and reached in the back seat for them.

"He fired and the shot hit the car door and ricocheted into my wife's foot," Mr. Mallott said.

He said, "Throw down tho-e

HARRY WEBB JR.
The description fit.

Crime continued to plague Spring. In one circumstance a decade after the bank robberies, Charlie Klein, Constable, received a knife wound when he sought to enforce the law in a "highway beer joint." Even in 1951, Spring had spurts of excitement. The audacious robbery of Bill and Dorothy Mallott in their own backyard made headlines. Sheriff C. V. (Buster) Kern apprehended the robber and recovered a portion of the stolen money.

been deputized—not knowing the courthouse was occupied, had taken aim at two traffic violators who escaped him as he brought them to the town jail. His barrage had cleared the court-

The remnants of Spring's old jail still exist by the railroad track on Border Street.

Above: The courthouse much as it appeared in Judge Doering's time. This building served a variety of purposes after the courthouse closed and the Harris County Courthouse for this section of the county was moved to a more central location. Today, the structure has been refurbished to house the Spring Historical Museum which opened in 1995.

not wood, was put in its place. A former Spring lawman describes Spring's jail: Conditions in the courtroom/ jail were "primitive" and there was "no air conditioning." The shell of that second little building still stands, condemned and no longer in use for thirty years.

The jail decayed and was lost, but one can still find records of it on old Harris County budgets in the Harris County Auditor's Office. For example, on December 31, 1955, as specified in 1955 budget allowances to jails in the county, the Spring jail was allocated $151.00. For 1956, the Spring jail received a budget of $177.00.

An interesting story about an earlier Spring jail comes from a Mr. Klein Westbrook of the Harris County Tax Office who remembers when his grandfather, Charlie Klein, was Constable of Spring. Westbrook says that at that time the jail was a train caboose. Every Saturday, the Constable took the prisoners in the caboose to jail in Houston. One of Westbrook's chores was to help with the cleaning and maintenance of the caboose jail. The

room; but what happened to the escaping criminals? Gertie does not remember.

That original wooden courthouse structure that harbored such memories fell down or was torn down, and another—almost a duplicate of the original—but constructed of cinder blocks,

Vernon Doering was the last Justice of the Peace in Spring. During the 1960's and early 1970's, Doering worked from a bonafide Harris County Courthouse established at the Y where Spring-Cypress splits into Main Street and Midway Street. The courthouse was the remodeled Church of Christ building.

RE-ELECT
JAMES G. WUNSCHE
JUSTICE OF THE PEACE
PRECINCT #7

YOUR SUPPORT AND VOTE WILL BE GRATEFULLY APPRECIATED

James Wunsche was Justice of the Peace in the late '50's in Spring. Judge Wunsche was the first Justice to operate from an office rather than from his home.

former location of the caboose jail is not specified.

Justices of the Peace in the early days of Spring, such as Karl (Charles) Holzwarth, were individuals summoned from their homes to perform their duties; they had no defined office or public place from which to operate. Spring's first Justice of the Peace office was established in the late 50's by James G. Wunsche. Wunsche's office building was located near the juncture of I-45 and Spring-Cypress Road. As Justice of the Peace, Wunsche held court in his office or in the old jail building.

Vernon Doering was the last Justice of the Peace in Spring. He had an office in his home and operated out of the "new courthouse," trying accused criminals, marrying couples, and handling a variety of judicial matters. Doering served in this capacity in the 60's and 70's. The "new courthouse" is now the home of the Spring Historical Museum.

Recognition for a Group of Spring Citizens

One group of Spring citizens, about whom little is mentioned in the histories, lived—and many still live— in an area bordered by Caroline and Hardy Streets and along Spring-Stuebner Road just north and west of the original town center of Spring. These were African-Americans who settled in an area referred to as the "quarters." Even though the term suggests plantation "slave quarters," and slaves were kept in Tomball and surrounding areas, there seems to be no mention of slavery in Spring itself. The settlement of black people probably originated with Freedmen who moved in with the railroad construction and stayed to work on the farms and in the mills, postulates Kessler in her *Narrative*

Spring's Masonic Lodge has always been an integral part of the community. Men of Spring Masonic Lodge #1174 AF&AM pose for a picture in the 1950's. From left to right, they are as follows: Watson Tomlinson; Jessie E. Robinson (son of R. L. Robinson); Homer Brown (teller at Spring State Bank during bank robberies in the '30's); George Tomlinson (known as Chad); Bartow Harper; Earl Wunsche, Sr. (Wunsche Motor Company and great grandson of Carl Wunsche, Sr.); J. O. Salyers ("Jimbo"; grandson of Dr. O. E. Robertson, Spring community doctor c. 1900); Willard Mallott, Sr. (Bill of Mallott's Grocery).

Born in Humble, Texas, on May 22, 1900, Dorothy Mallott and her husband Bill moved to Spring in 1936. They operated a grocery store on Main Street until 1970. Mrs. Mallott is known for her charitable acts and for her needlework. At more than one hundred years of age, she still sews sunbonnets.

Gertie Mae Duce Salyers moved to Spring with her family in 1923. She graduated from the two-story brick school at the end of Spring School Road in 1926. She and her husband Jimbo are remembered for their work with public education in Spring. Salyers Elementary School is named in their honor. Mrs. Salyers works as a volunteer in the Spring Historical Museum. Her birthday is August 9, 1908.

Ethnography of Spring. Early black families with names such as Thomas, Summerville, Dockins, and King bought land in this area and sold the land to others. The "quarters" area is as old as the town itself; Spring's first church was formed there in 1885.

For about seventy years, the people of the "quarters" were isolated and self-sufficient. They worked alongside whites, harvesting crops in the fields and cutting timber for the mills, but when the workday was over, each ethnicity went its separate way. The black families traded at the local mercantiles, but they also had their own businesses, spent social time together, went to school, and attended church with their own. They were a hardworking and honest people who enjoyed their Saturday night blues and their Sunday morning gospel singing. A complete history, specifically recognizing the contributions and accomplishments of Spring's black Americans, has yet to be recorded. Only with school integration in the 1960's did the two predominate races of Spring begin to mingle socially. White and black youth studied together in the classroom, and they played together on the various athletic teams. Parents cheered together at the Friday night game. The power of Texas football, as much as any other factor, served as the force that finally brought black and white together in Spring.

The Need to Change the Town's Image

In a return to the chronology of the town: Old Spring had a fleeting, often rough, golden hour. As evidenced here, much is made of the turbulent lifestyle in early Spring. One of the most poignant testimonies to Spring's moral turpitude comes in the form of a letter written by a Mr. and Mrs. McClanahan, who ran the Sellers Hotel, to their landlords J. C. and Julia Sellers. In the letter, the McClanahans state their regret at having to give up the hotel, yet they feel they cannot stay in the decadence of Spring any longer. The letter continues:

It has been the one desire of our lives every since we lost our boy at Spring, to live there,

George "See Doc" Pruitt, a true gentleman, in a photo from his earlier years. Doc lived a long and fruitful life— December 28, 1902—March 29, 1998: ninety-six years. Doc was often called the "Mayor" of Spring because he managed to stay in touch with so many people in the area for so many years. His obituary reads: "A community person, he went every day while he could, helping people to meet their needs. He was a happy man who was kind and considerate of everyone. . . . He encouraged everyone to stay on the right road." Here is a line from a poem written in his honor:

"So many owed so much to him,
He had become a part of the history of Spring."

and remain the balance of our lives, in the place where he left us, but the hotel patronage at Spring is made up of people among whom decency and morality has ceased to be a virtue, and integrity of character a reward, and therefore we must forego the most cherished hope of our lives.

Even though the railroad and the sawmills attracted many transients and riffraff who jaded the town with their "hard-livin,' hard-drinkin'" revelry, practical citizens wanted to bring in a more settled clientele: "a *family audience.*" The Spring Chamber of Commerce stationary publicized the area as follows: "Spring has: Pure

Lelia (Aunt Lee) Pennington can tell many stories of Spring, Texas, during the '40's and '50's. She lived in downtown Spring and worked at Spring Cafe from 1949 to 1955. April 14, 1909, is her birthday. Mrs. Pennington is the town poet and songwriter, and she hopes some day to have her work published. Her song "Christmas in Old Town Spring" has been set to music. Here are samples of selected lyrics:

Oh there'll be a Merry Christmas *Down in Old Town Spring.* *Christmas bells ringing,* *In Old Town Spring.*	*Singing and dancing* *Up and down the street* *Music will be playing* *To an old Christmas beat.*
Shops decorated in *Red, white, and green.* *Upon the Christmas tree* *So many things to be seen.*	*Lights burning* *Shining so bright.* *Down in Old Town Spring* *On Christmas night.*

Artesian Water, Several Churches, Good Schools and Fine Farm Lands. [Spring is] not too far away from the Gulf to get the sea breezes but far enough inland to be safe from the Gulf storms. The sea breeze makes a delightful climate, winter and summer."

Sensationalism speaks in a strident voice; goodness is mild, but pervasive all the same when one uncovers it. Churches certainly made Spring a favorable place to live.

Churches Involved in the Development of the Town of Spring

History of worship in North Harris Country may be traced through various early churches such as Trinity Lutheran Church of Klein, founded in 1874; Westfield Methodist Church, founded in 1893; and St. Matthew's Lutheran Church, founded in 1886. Worship in Spring may be delineated by looking at the following:

ST. PAUL UNITED METHODIST CHURCH

The oldest church in the area is St. Paul United Methodist Church, established in 1885. The history of the church, outlined in St. Paul's 110 year anniversary booklet, attributes the donation of the property for St. Paul to the Fuzzle family. The first place of worship was a wood-frame church on Booker Drive, just behind the present sanctuary. Since then, St. Paul has had a series of worship centers. The first wooden building was replaced with another wooden building, then a tile and cement structure, and finally in 1965, the present modern structure. The congregation, led by Rev. C. L. Polk III, remains viable and an important part of the community. The dedication in St. Paul's anniversary program lauds the founders of the church:

> We are dedicating this program to the pioneers of St. Paul. . . . They had very little money, they came to church walking, on horse-back, in wagons, in the rain and cold.

St. Paul United Methodist Church, established in 1885, is the oldest church in the Spring area.

Sometimes they couldn't pay the preacher. They would give him vegetables out of their gardens, or meat they had cured. . . .

Good old St. Paul: We had some testifying, shouting, powerful praying and singing time here on this ground. Thank God for our pioneers . . . .

TRUEVINE MISSIONARY BAPTIST CHURCH

St. Paul's neighbor, Truevine Missionary Baptist Church at 27307 Oak Street, was established in 1902 with less than fifty members. A gift of property from the King family provided a place for Truevine's first sanctuary, originally located at 314 Booker Street. When the church felt the need for a more modern building, the congregation purchased two lots on Oak Street; and members worked diligently to raise money for construction of a new physical plant. Under the leadership of Rev. Godwin Haynes, the church has continued to improve its facilities. In 1995, Truevine marked ninety-three years of service with an anniversary service and a commemorative booklet. Rev. Eddie Jones, chairman of the souvenir book, writes in the Foreword of the booklet a description of the church's enduring spirit:

In retrospect, we members of the True-

Truevine Missionary Baptist Church dates from 1902.

vine Missionary Baptist Church visualize a small body of baptized believers organizing a church more than 93 years ago with only a few members and no house; we see this band of Christian workers struggle to erect a small monument, though it met the need of the day. . . .

The world has turned over many times since that eventful year 1902, but Truevine has at all times lifted the high banner . . . .

The congregation of Truevine Missionary Baptist Church posed for this picture sometime in the late 1950's. The backdrop is the old Truevine Church building.

THE UNION CHURCH

In 1909, the Methodist Episcopal Church, South, received from J. C. Sellers an acre of land upon which a wood frame church was constructed. A German Lutheran congregation also conducted church services in the building. The Baptist Church initially did not own a facility for its worship, and it too conducted church services in the Methodist Church building. When the three churches held joint services, the church was known as the "Union Church." Two of these churches, Spring Baptist Church and Immanuel United Church, continue to exist as lively congregations in the Spring area.

The Union Church sat on Aldine-Westfield Road on land donated by Mr. and Mrs. J. C. Sellers. The building served three denominations, hence the name "Union Church." A Methodist congregation, a Lutheran congregation that became Immanuel United Church, and Spring Baptist Church all met in this building.

SPRING BAPTIST CHURCH

Spring Baptist Church originated in 1913 in the Union Church building on Aldine-Westfield Road. Following a revival in which a young, dynamic pastor, Rev. Dale Crowley, converted many, the congregation outgrew the Union Church building and relocated in 1925 in the heart of downtown Spring on Midway Street. The locale on Aldine-Westfield became the worship spot of a Pentecostal church. On February 17, 1945, when Bertha West Hamblin

Spring's largest church, Spring Baptist Church, has more than 4,000 members and continues to grow as the area attracts more people. Frequently, Spring Baptist Church is involved in building expansion in order to maintain facilities to accommodate its ever-increasing numbers!

conveyed to the Baptist Church Lots 5, 6, and 9, Block 1 of the Robinson Addition, the church expanded in its downtown location. The wooden church was removed and a cinderblock sanctuary was constructed in its place. This building still stands in its original location on Midway Street where it is used for a variety of Old Town Spring shops.

Always a burgeoning congregation, Spring Baptist Church built a larger church at its present location on Spring-Cypress Road and Lexington Boulevard. At this site, the church has had three different sanctuaries, each larger than the other, to accommodate its ever-expanding numbers of worshippers. Even today, the church has another building project underway! The congregation now has more than four thousand members and sponsors a Spanish-speaking congregation of 135 in a nearby building.

IMMANUEL UNITED CHURCH

The Lutherans of Spring met in the Union Church and in members' homes from a time in 1913. Anxious to establish an official church,

Chartered in 1916 with the name Deutsche Evangelisch Lutherischen Immanuels Gemeinde Zu Spring, *Immanuel United Church derived from a Lutheran denomination brought to the United States with German immigrants.*

the congregation of first- and second-generation German families filed a charter on July 15, 1916, with the state of Texas in the name *Deutsche Evangelisch Lutherischen Immanuels Gemeinde Zu Spring.* Translated, the name in English is "German Evangelical Lutheran Emmanuels Congregation at Spring, Texas." The members built a small, white church at the corner of Spring-Cypress Road and Border Street on 1.53 acres, purchased from R. L. Robinson for $114.75. Influential gentlemen of the area served as charter members: Frank Arp, Louis Benignus, George Goedecke, Charles Holzwarth, Charles Klein, Henry Kothman, Eli Lemm, Egenhardt Strack, and Herman Strack. In 1948, on adjacent land donated by R. L. Robinson and his wife, Mary Ehrhardt Robinson, the church built a parish hall to serve its parishioners—and the community. The parish hall was a community project: church members donated the lumber and the labor; Bayer Lumber Company dried the lumber and planed it as a gift to the church. When the hall was completed, barbecues and other social functions kept the building filled.

In February of 1953, first the parish hall, and then the frame church, caught fire one Sunday night. People of Spring rushed to save the original stained glass windows, pews, and anything movable from the building. With no fire equipment available, in spite of valiant efforts, the buildings burned to the ground. Later in 1953, the congregation rebuilt on the

same location a brick church which still stands. One gift for the Immanuel sanctuary was from R. W. Duce, who donated the old Spring school bell to the church. To this day on Sunday morning, the bell that called Spring children to class long ago calls worshippers to Immanuel Church. The congregation has seen mergers with other denominations and now goes by the name of Immanuel United Church.

SPRING CHURCH OF CHRIST

Spring Church of Christ organized with twelve families in 1935. Pioneers in the church were sisters Carrie Brill and Ima Blair, who led Bible studies in their home; and Seth Walker and Ebb Bonds, who served as elders and helped to enlarge the congregation. This dedicated group first met in the wooden community building owned by the Woodmen of the World, on Aldine-Westfield Road. In 1942, the congregation built a small church on East Hardy Road. The church flourished because of strong members and great spirituality.

The Church of Christ had a serious problem. The small building lacked a baptistry. One member declares, "The favorite location for baptisms by the congregation in Spring was Spring Creek near the bridge on Riley Fuzzel Road. . . . The creek provided pleasant memories for summer days, [but in the winter] the water [was] cold, and had ice in it as well. Now that's a strong belief in the need for baptism."

Spring Church of Christ on Spring-Cypress Road is the first church to greet visitors on their way to Old Town Spring. This church began its organization in 1935.

Later, in 1950, the Church of Christ built in Spring at the Y intersection of Spring-Cypress and Midway, partly with lumber from an old oil tank that had been torn down next to the railroad track. Harris County bought the church building in 1967 to renovate and use as a local courthouse. (This building now houses the Spring Historical Museum.) When this transaction occurred, Spring Church of Christ constructed its present sanctuary on Spring-Cypress just east of I-45. An excellent history of this church and of the surrounding Spring area may be found in the publication *The First Fifty Years: A History of the Spring Church of Christ,* a booklet produced by the church in 1988.

Many wonderful churches surround Spring and contribute to the spiritual life of area residents, but the aforementioned are directly rooted in the early development of the town and should be documented as part of "Spring's history."

Spring Schools and School Personnel

From the earliest days, Spring citizens have been continually on a quest for better schools. The first log school the German settlers erected "was blown off its blocks and . . . . abandoned," writes Maxine Moore for the *1960 Sun*. It was replaced by another school building—and another.

Initially, Spring schools were part of Common School District #4. However, according to John Robinson, "In September 1907, the town selected to become an independent school district. . . ." As small schools consolidated in this new school district comprised of 24.96 square miles, the community built "a new building . . . on the old Sellers estate, just across the track in Spring on Aldine-Westfield Road." The original school trustees, in addition to the aforementioned R. L. Robinson, were A. Bender, George Goedecke, Charlie Klein, H. A. Minze, Henry West, and William Wunsche, Sr.

Eighteen children of the Spring area pose against their wooden school building. The picture tells about rural schooling anywhere in the United States in the early twentieth century, not just Spring. The children are of a variety of sizes and ages, ranging from the tiny girl in front to the older boys and girls on the back row, yet just one teacher poses with them, indicating of course that all levels are taught by the one lady! (Teachers, this educator is the expert on how to accommodate the individual learner!) As can best be determined in the aged picture, only four of the eighteen children are boys. Perhaps the other boys have withdrawn from school to get jobs or to work at home. Or perhaps they have just been kept home for the day to help with chores that must be done.

— Courtesy of John Robinson

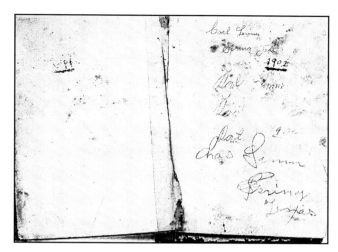

Even though German families were anxious that their children learn English, some education in Spring's first schools may have occurred in German, either as the primary language or as the second language. What appears to be a German schoolbook, published in 1898, is signed by Carl Lemm (or Charles Lemm) in 1902. Lemm attended six years of school at the Spring School Annex.

— Courtesy of Diana Haude

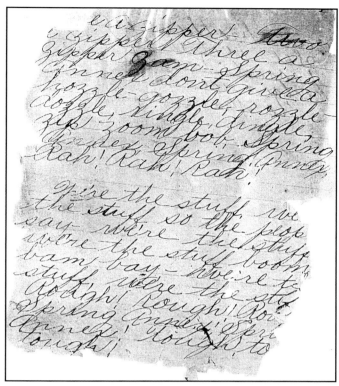

School spirit exists in most schools, no matter the type or size. Evidence of that may be found in Dora Lemm's note-book that she kept during her school days at one of the Spring Schools, the Spring School Annex on Aldine-Westfield Road. Here is an Annex cheer in Dora's handwriting. We do not know if Dora has simply copied the school's words or if she, as a creative young woman, has written an exaltation of the school on her own. The handwritten text dates from c. 1902.

— Courtesy of Laverne Lemm Henry

One of the early Spring schools about which much remains is the "Spring Annex School" or the "Schultz School." To establish a school in the Schultz Settlement along Aldine-Westfield Road, the school district, on February 8, 1912, acquired from Henry Schultz and wife Annie a one-acre tract of land in the Ambrose Mays Survey. Using a team of longhorn steers, Henry Schultz moved an old school building across the railroad tracks to the one-acre section of land. Local farmers Schultz and Otto Meyer were acting trustees for the school, and in addition Meyer had the responsibility of providing the school with heater wood and of replacing broken windows damaged by careless students. The Schultz family boarded the teachers for the school.

Comments of former Annex students tell of conditions that contrast vastly with school life and regulations today. One Annex student Richard Meyer tells of how he was permitted to skip the ninth month of school to work on the family farm. Even though he missed the end of school, he was not penalized: he was promoted to the next grade each year. Avalt Meyer, Richard's brother, recalls that drinking water for the school was carried from the Henry Schultz well. Students took turns going to the well for water, walking through high grass and weeds on their treks to and from the schoolhouse. Commonly, grasshoppers fell into the water bucket, and the grasshoppers had to be strained from the water to make it fit for drinking because the "girls didn't like the look of those grasshoppers drowning in the water," says Avalt. Leona Schultz Bayer remembers the wood-frame school building with outside "privy" and no running water. She also recalls that the janitorial duties were passed on to the female students, who had the responsibility of sweeping the school each day.

On one occasion, the school caught fire, and all rushed to put out the fire, many carrying buckets of water laced with iron ore from Schultz Gully. Otto Meyer went on the roof of the school with an axe to cut a hole and pour water on the fire. The school was saved, but Otto's son Richard Meyer, who was not nearly

To serve a growing, thriving town, in 1918 the Spring School District contracted Oscar Holcomb, who later became mayor of Houston, to build a two-story brick school. The building held ten, then eleven, grades; older grades, upstairs; younger children, downstairs.

— Courtesy of Spring I.S.D. Archives

as concerned as his father, says "I said let it burn down so I won't have to go to school!"

Nevertheless, the Annex persevered, as did the children—who often came to school under difficult conditions. Spring students on the east end of Treschwig Road had to cross a corner of the Aldine School District to reach Spring Annex School. The Hildebrandt children—Herman, Walter, Clara, and Ruby—walked five miles to school or rode horseback until the last year of school when they had the luxury of riding to school in the family car, a Model T Ford.

Gladys Hildebrandt Tullos, in her article "For the Love of Education," writes of her father's school days at the Annex. She says:

Walter, my dad, and about nine other kids including his sisters and brother, had to walk five miles one way to school each day. . . . He took pancakes or biscuits and salt bacon in his lunch. His lunch pail was a syrup bucket, and he had to carry a pocket knife to open it. One day his teacher took his knife away from him. Dad was so bashful he never asked the teacher to open his lunch bucket for him.

In those days teachers were very strict and used a big paddle quite frequently.

Teachers may have been strict at the Annex,

but they must have engendered respect. Avalt Meyer rescued his teacher's chair from the old Annex school and kept it for years, finally donating the chair to the Spring Historical Museum as a momento of his school days. Avalt's teacher was Linda Kaiser Baumgartner. Other teachers at the Annex were Joe Dunnam, who was the first teacher; Bertie Barton; Dorothy Darden; Sadie Laird; Minnie Laird; Ethel Lee Heitman; Sue Davis; and Elsie Smith.

Dora Schultz Lemm had quite an affection for the Annex when she was a school girl there in the early 1900's. In her notebook, Dora recorded a school "cheer" or "pep chant." Whether she created the cheer, or the chant was used by the entire school, is not clear. Dora writes (Punctuation is Dora's):

One a zipper two a zipper three a zipper zam
Spring Annex dont give a hozzle-gozzle, rozzle-dozzle, ringle-dingle zip zoom bob
Spring Annex, Spring Annex, Rah! Rah! Rah!
We're the stuff, we're the stuff, so the people say—
We're the stuff boom bam bay
We're the stuff
Rough! Rough! Rough!

Spring Annex! Spring Annex!
Tough! tough! tough! tough!

If one interprets Dora's attitude correctly, school spirit was not lacking at the Annex!

Just as the Spring citizens in the "quarters" established strong churches for their community, they also had schools for their children. An excellent source for information on education in the black community is Mr. B. F. Clark, twelve-year principal of Southwell (1951-1963), the Spring School for Black Students. In terms of his background, Mr. Clark started to college in 1936 and began his teaching career in 1938 with a four-year temporary Texas Teacher's Certificate. When World War II interrupted his work, Clark served three and a half years in the United States Army, part of that time on Iwo Jima. At his discharge as a decorated sergeant,

Clark had been awarded two Bronze Stars among other honors for distinguished service. After he left the army, Mr. Clark gave himself totally to the education of Texas children. He earned a Master's Degree from Prairie View College in 1949 and came to Spring, Texas, in 1951. Through interviews and research, Mr. Clark has compiled a paper on the history of schooling in the black community. He records the following:

> I have not been able to locate anyone who can give me the exact date of the beginning of the black school. However, Mrs. Beatrice McGowen [Burks], who began school in 1910, attended a one-room school located at the corner of Elm and Magnolia Streets. Therefore, 1910 may be a possible anniversary year for the first black school in Spring.

In 1918, when the white population had

One of the first groups of children to study in the new school, this class is arranged against the brick side of the building. Dressed in their "Sunday best," the boys wear shoes, coats, and pullover sweater vests. The girls' hair is bobbed, some hair skewed back with big bows. Adaline Kreinhop is the fifth child on the second row, a little blond girl with a bow. Three children over from Adaline on the right, a small girl is wedged between two of the bigger girls. The teacher's child? A baby sister come to visit school? Perhaps so, since little brothers and sisters were allowed to visit at school during this time. Or is she the photographer's baby? Ahh! the puzzling details of wonderful old pictures!

— Courtesy of Sandra Kreinhop Sheffield

Mr. B. F. Clark, twelve-year principal of Southwell (1951-1963), the Spring School for Black Students, has compiled a history of schooling in the black schools. Mr. Clark remembers vividly the integration of Spring schools. An elementary school in the Spring Independent School District has been named for Mr. Clark.

outgrown its school on Aldine-Westfield Road, the school building was moved to the black settlement with a team of oxen. This larger building would accommodate the expanding group of black children. One of the early educators in the black community was Mr. W. M. Southwell, who served as principal of the school for black children for twenty years. In 1951, the school in the black community burned and was replaced by a brick building which in the late '50's or early '60's was named Southwell School in honor of Mr. Southwell's years of service.

One account of a Spring school (with no date) is a description of a building on or near Elm Street in the area of town where black families lived—a school building, forty foot by forty foot, partitioned down the center, with black children being taught on one side and white children, on the other. Earl Wunsche and Paul Klein attended school in this building. According to John Robinson, the board of trustees at that time was a group of four, and as decreed by the county was composed of two black and two white representatives.

Mrs. Beatrice Burks, mentioned earlier, who is ninety-seven, remembers attending school at a location near Spring Road and Hardy Street in the "quarters." However, she has no recollection of a school serving blacks and whites together. She only remembers that the location for the school was different from the present site.

To serve a still growing, thriving town, the Spring School District replaced the building it had moved from the Aldine-Westfield Road site with a new brick school on the same location. The contractor who built this eight-room, two-storied school, designed to hold grades one through ten, two grades per room, was Oscar Holcomb. For those who have been here long enough to remember: Oscar Holcomb was destined to become Mayor of Houston.

August Wunsche has vivid recollections of his school days at the red brick school. As a small boy, August walked to school, but when August was twelve years old in 1924, his father bought a Model T touring car. From that time until his graduation in 1929, August drove the touring car to school from his home on Spring

August Wunsche remembers his days in the Spring School at the end of Spring School Road. August walked to school as a small child; then when he was twelve years old, he was allowed to drive his father's new Model T Touring Car to school—from a location on Spring-Stuebner Road, a distance of about five miles. August's birthday is July 17, 1912. August Wunsche is a decorated veteran of World War II, a gentleman who savors history and who generously shares his memories of early Spring life.

Carl Wunsche High School was established in 1938, on land donated by the Wunsche Family.

Stuebner Road. Other children were not so fortunate as August, who drove his own car at age twelve; they rode on a bus that Willie Wunsche and others built from a used Model T Ford truck—Spring's first school bus.

On Armistice Day, November 11, 1918, the day marking the end of World War I, Spring school children left the block-style, brick school building and celebrated just as all children in the United States did. School was dismissed early, and the children marched around the town, singing patriotic songs and rejoicing that the fighting in Europe was over.

Gladys Tullos reveals other memories of school days, this time her own in 1945 in the brick building on Aldine-Westfield at the end of Spring School Road. Tullos recalls:

> I can remember when I started school at Spring. . . . It was a two story building. the enrollment was so small that the first and second grades were in the same classroom, and only two buses were needed to transport the entire student body.
>
> Mr. W. F. (Buck) Hoffmann drove one school bus and his son, William, drove the other. . . .
>
> [When] I was a first grader, there was no school cafeteria; therefore everyone had to take a lunch.
>
> I cannot remember the second story of the school being used for anything except

storing books and nurses giving shots to the school children. . . . I can still smell the alcohol, when I think of it, and still remember us lining up and so many kids crying and others asking, "Did it hurt?"

> There was a big heater in the classroom, but I cannot remember whether it burned wood or coal. The teacher would appoint certain boys to keep the fire going.

From 1917 to 1934, Charles P. McLachlan, a prominent figure in Spring education, served as Superintendent of Schools. Mr. McLachlan was also on the Board of Trustees for the school district.

Children from rural areas were bussed to school in vehicles like the one shown here. In this 1930 photograph, Britt Harris is the bus driver.

— Courtesy of John Robinson

The consolidation of several rural districts with Spring resulted in increased growth in the Spring Independent School District. In 1935, under the direction of Superintendent James H. Goettee, the school district gained state accreditation. In 1938, Spring built a new high school, Carl Wunsche Sr. High School, on land donated by Carl Wunsche. For one year, Willard Frandolog became superintendent, the same year the new high school opened. A local witness remembers that the students were transferred to the new school in unique fashion. The students were told to assemble their personal belongings, notebooks, and books. Then, with these items in hand, the students walked the mile from the old brick school on Aldine-Westfield to the new brick school on Spring Cypress Road! The school change had been effected in expedient fashion.

As the superintendent with the longest tenure, John A. Winship served the Spring schools thirty-four years (1939-1973). During his years with the District, the Spring school system expanded from three schools into a powerful school district in populous North Harris County. Mr. Winship served the District as teacher, coach, worker, builder, and superintendent.

John A. Winship, Superintendent of Spring Independent School District, 1939-1973. The Winships—John and Pearl—have been honored by the Spring District: Winship Elementary School was named for this pair who served the schools so faithfully.

When the old brick school on Aldine-Westfield was condemned and closed, the District, in 1947, constructed Spring Elementary School adjacent to the high school. The building housed children in grades one through seven.

School integration occurred in the sixties—1966 to be exact. All black children, including the eleventh and twelfth grade black students who had been transferred to Carver High School in Aldine ISD because there were no facilities for them at Southwell, entered Wunsche High School and Spring Elementary School. Mr. Clark recalls the days of integration in Spring and applauds the smooth procedure which brought black children into white schools in the District. He says the assimilation occurred in steps: in 1962, the eleventh and twelfth grade black youth entered Spring High School. Other grades followed, and by 1966, integration had been completed. Clark remembers no difficulty in the process; he says that all the Southwell staff went into the Spring ISD system, continued to teach, and eventually retired from the Spring schools. The Southwell facility has since been converted into a community center. Those who want more details about the school district, its early years, and its expansion, may visit the Spring Schools Museum in Wunsche School on Spring-Cypress Road.

The Spring Independent School District now covers fifty-seven miles which include a population of about 115,000 people. The District has an enrollment of more than 22,000 students in fifteen elementary schools, four middle schools, two 5A high schools, and one community school—which is housed in the refurbished Carl Wunsche High School. Certainly, the School District has outstripped the original community, and the two are no longer one and the same.

Doctors and Medical Services

Churches and schools often keep historical records. But an area of service, such as medicine and health care, may lack specific documentation. Spring is no exception. The first medical services were, no doubt, as scarce as they were in most rural areas. One of Spring's first doctors, Dr. O. E. Robertson, who had a store in early Spring, made rounds to treat those who were ill and to deliver babies. Gertie Mae Salyers, whose husband was related to Dr. Robertson, shares her memories of Robertson. Robertson, pharmacist and physician, took his payment in whatever form he could get it: cash, vegetables, chickens, or eggs.

Early in the century, Dr. T. E. Dunham established Dunham Hospital in Spring for railroad personnel and for other townspeople. As the hospital doctor there in 1902 and for years after, Dunham had no easy job. Injuries during these times could be gruesome—heavy equipment, propelled by men and horses, could slip and fall on workers—labor in the roundhouse, on the trains, or on the railroad tracks was dangerous. Stories abound about railroad injuries: John Robinson says that "the president of the railroad company was actually killed in a construction accident right at Spring when the railroad was being built." The son of one of Spring's prominent families, Willie Klein—a young husband with an infant daughter—was crushed in a railroad accident. According to Jesse Vaughn, who researched the history of the Holzwarth family, Carl Holzwarth, German immigrant, farmer, Justice of the Peace, and railroad worker, had "a scar below the right cheekbone," the remains of an injury he received "while working for the railroad when a coal bucket hit him in the face accidentally."

Work for the sawmills was no less dangerous: cutting, loading, and dressing timber in the woods and at the mills brought heightened risk of accident and maiming. Just as the shrill blast from a coal mine in a mining town signaled a disaster at the mine so did the repeated scream of Bayer's mill whistle let Spring citizens know an accident had occurred in the mill or in the woods.

Appropriately, here we should digress with an anecdote from Arthur Bayer about medical practices at the Spring Hospital. Arthur Bayer is Spring's Renaissance man: retired from Bayer Mill—owner of Spring's water works—supervisor of sundry Spring properties—Spring historian—former chief of the Spring Volunteer Fire Department—Chemical Engineer in World War II—graduate of Southwestern University in 1941 with a degree in Chemical Engineering and Mathematics. Having come to Spring in

Dr. O. E. Robertson as he might appear on his rounds, his medical bag in hand.

— Courtesy of Gertie Mae Salyers

1927 as a child, Bayer has heard about, or has witnessed, many events in the life of this town and its people. Bayer remembers hearing of medical cases at Dunham's hospital. He recalls that his own grandfather, Dr. Theodore Laut, a surgeon, helped Dr. Dunham at the hospital with critical cases in which a patient with an injury or a damaged limb might require special treatment or amputation. To assist in treatment, Dr. Laut traveled to Spring from his home in Rose Hill, west of Tomball, by horse and buggy. Laut brought his surgical tools with him, but on occasion Dr. Laut might be detained at home or the doctors might need other equipment. Under these conditions, doctors called the local butcher, a Mr. Windy Lee, skilled in cutting and sawing sides of beef, from his butcher shop to aid, if amputation were needed.

In addition to his work at the hospital, Dunham, ever true to the Hippocratic Oath,

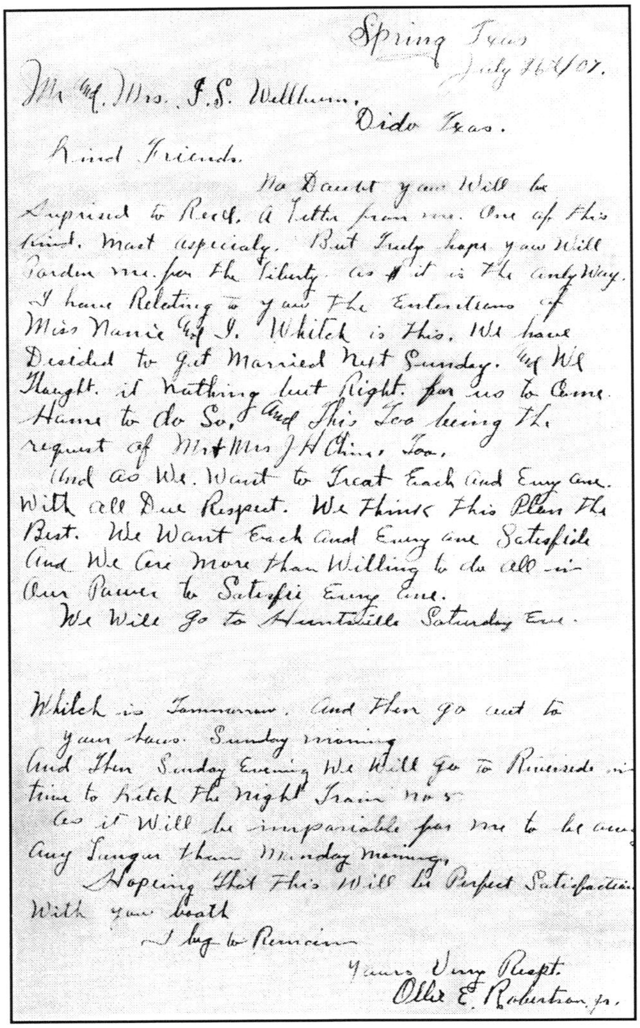

[Handwritten letter reproduced]

> Spring Texas
> July 26/07.
>
> Mr & Mrs. J. S. Welburn,
> Dido Texas.
>
> Kind Friends.
>
> No Doubt you Will be Suprised to Rec'd. a letter from me. One of this kind. Most especialy. But Truly hope you Will Pardon me for the liberty. as if it is the only Way. I have Relating to you The Ententions of Miss Nannie & I. Whitch is this. We have Decided to get Married Next Sunday. & We Thought it nothing but Right for us to Come Home to do So, & This Too being the request of Mr & Mrs J H China, Too.
>
> And as We Want to Treat Each and Every One. With all Due Respect. We Think This Plan the Best. We Want Each and Every one Satisfied And We are More than Willing to do all in Our Power to Satisfie Every One. We Will go to Huntsville Saturday Eve.
>
> Whitch is Tomorrow. And Then go out to your Home Sunday morning And Then Sunday Evening We Will go to Riverside in time to Ketch the night Train no 5 as it Will be imposiable for me to be over Any longer than Monday morning. Hopeing That This Will be Perfect Satisfaction With your Self.
>
> I beg to Remain
> Yours Very Respt.
> Ollie E. Robertson Jr.

Dr. Robertson's son, O. E. (Ollie) Robertson, Jr. joined his father in the family business in Spring. In 1907, he married Nannie Welburn. Here is the letter he wrote on July 26 to Nannie's parents, announcing the marriage plans. Notice that the prospective bride and groom will be traveling partly by train to and from the home of the bride's parents. They plan to take the night train from Riverside, outside of Huntsville, back to Spring.

— Courtesy of Clay Mills

attended to medical needs of the town by means of house calls. Gertie Salyers, recalls when, as a young girl, she was treated by Dr. Dunham, who made a house call to her aunt's house to attend her. Young James Wunsche, Willie and Earl's brother, chauffeured Dr. Dunham on his various rounds. In fact, Wunsche got his driver's license so that he could fulfill his duties as the doctor's chauffeur. Because Dunham had such a large territory and such a serious job, the doctor seemed dauntless and would do anything to

treat those who were ill. Once, when the Spring Creek bridge was flooded, and there was no way to get across the swollen waterway to a particular case of his, Dunham had James Wunsche to drive out to the railroad bridge that spanned the creek. When a train came to cross the bridge, Dunhan, determined to get to his patient, hitched a ride on the engine's cowcatcher and rode across the trestle, clinging precariously to the front of the train. Wunsche waited by his jitney and, much later, watched as Dunham returned on a south bound train, again hanging to the engine in the same way, until he reached the safety of his car and driver. One would wish for more information about the colorful Dr. Dunham: John Robinson says Dunham was also a Baptist preacher, filling a pulpit in a church near Bammel every other Sunday of the month!

Dr. J. C. Sellers, a doctor—and a Spring businessman—made his house calls, too. His daughter, Natalene Sellers remembered going with her father to the home of Riley Fuzzel, who lived in a ranch house at the end of the Spring-New Caney Road, later to be known as Riley Fuzzel Road, once to treat Fuzzel's children, who had a fever, and another time to deliver Fuzzel's youngest child.

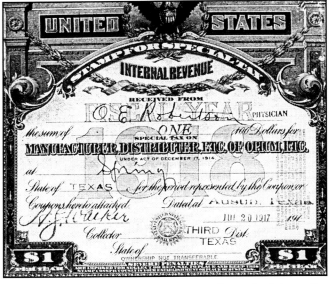

Doctors served as pharmacists as well as physicians. Dr. Robertson was required to take great care in his role as druggist in the community. This receipt verifies the one dollar special tax on opium and related drugs Robertson paid to the Internal Revenue Service. For this tax, Robertson could distribute opium to those in need.

— Courtesy of Gertie Mae Salyers

A family picture of the Robertson family made in 1907. On the back row is Nannie Wellburn Robertson. She stands next to her husband, O. E. Robertson, Jr. Robertson's sister, Jessie Lee Robertson Salyers, who married John Salyers, is beside him. On the front row is Dr. Robertson, his wife Hepsy Goodrum Robertson, and their grandson, James Oliver Salyers. James Oliver, or Jimbo as he came to be called, married Gertie Mae Duce.

— Courtesy of Clay Mills

Below: *After paying the tax, a doctor could order "opium or coca leaves, or compounds, manufactures, salts, derivatives or preparations thereof" from the United States Treasury Department. This form records Robertson's September 14, 1928, order for morphine.*

— Courtesy of Gertie Mae Salyers

Dr. E. O. Boggs, President of the Spring Chamber of Commerce in 1926, served as railroad doctor, pharmacist, and Spring community physician during the '20's and '30's. Having graduated from St. Louis College of Physicians and Surgeons, Boggs moved to Spring primarily to serve the railroad personnel, but he was also a general practitioner in the town. For a time, he used the brick drugstore on Midway as his office; he also used the little bank building after the bank moved, as his place of practice. Dr. Boggs treated the ill and injured, and if a person needed further aid, he took them or sent them on to a hospital in Houston. The first child Dr. Boggs delivered in the Spring area was Karl Theiss, Jr. on February 2, 1925. The second infant he delivered was a girl, Lydia Benignus, born September 23, 1925. To add a romantic note to a town's stories that are often violent or tragic: in February 1943, Karl Junior and Lydia Benignus, brought together by mutual friends, were married, learning later they had shared a similar natal experience. All their lives Junior and Lydia have lived near Spring on Budde Cemetery Road, rearing three daughters, staying close to what has always been home. These two who drew their first breaths in the hands of the same doctor have now (in the year 2001) lived together fifty-eight years.

Dr. E. O. Boggs poses in front of his office and drug store on Midway Street. The building was originally Dr. Dunham's Drug Store. Later, the brick structure served as a grocery store operated by Mel Brink and as a hardware store for Willard Mallott, Jr. Boggs pauses in his morning ritual of sweeping the front stoop to allow for a photograph. Later, Boggs practiced in the bank building, then in his home. The date for this photo is unknown.

— Courtesy of Naomi Boggs Thoms

The first child Dr. Boggs delivered when he came to Spring was Karl Theiss, Jr. The second infant he delivered in Spring was Lydia Benignus. Karl and Lydia were married in 1943, not knowing they shared "birth stories" until some time later.

Certain women with skill in delivering children served in and around the Spring area. The mid-wife in the "quarters" was Mrs. Victoria Lindsay. Mrs. Lindsay, who died in 1959, delivered most of the black children in the town. Her granddaughter, Laura Slaughter, has vivid memories of her grandmother and plans to write a book about Lindsay's eventful life. According to one source, another lady, Sophronia Wunsche—Mrs. William Wunsche, Sr.—often assisted doctors on medical cases. Whether Mrs. Wunsche was a mid-wife or a physician's assistant to one doctor or to all is not clear, but no one argues that she was often present at the births of children in the community. In fact, Mrs. Wunsche probably attended the doctors that delivered her own grandchildren.

This Spring shop is housed in the building Dunham and then Boggs operated as a drug store—the same building Boggs stands in front of in the previous picture. The dark structure next door with bars on the windows is the former post office of Spring. Mr. and Mrs. Will Horn and genial Bernard Strack served as postmasters in this building in the '40's and '50's. The light-colored building behind the automobile is the Spring Bank building, where two holdups and shootouts occurred in the early 1930's.

After Dr. Boggs moved away, Spring was left without a local physician; for a brief period of time, Dr. Norman Graham from Tomball had an office in the building north of Wunsche Motors. More often than not, until the 1970's, when a medical clinic opened on Spring-Cypress, people had to travel to nearby towns for medical needs.

The Loss of the Roundhouse: The Beginning of Spring's Decline

Spring's prosperity continued into the 1920's until the town faced two devastating circumstances: in 1919, Prohibition occurred, causing the saloons to close; and in 1923, the roundhouse moved away—to Houston. Reasons given for the departure of the railroad vary.

Some blame the German farmers and their love of the land for the railroad's move. Originally, the first- and second-generation Germans and the railroad personnel forged a happy union, railroad money nurturing the still-German town and daughters of the German families marrying the prosperous men of the railroad. Old wedding pictures still around today testify to such unions. Yet, these sources say, the railroad (in 1923 the Missouri Pacific Railroad), wanted more land to expand its roundhouse and yards, and the German farmers, who loved their land almost as much as they loved their daughters, would not sell. Perhaps, as a result of this overwhelming desire to keep land, the town lost its greatest patron.

Others who ponder on the loss of the railroad business in Spring have a different story. They say that the railroad left town for extended business opportunities. Spring did not offer the volume of activity the railroad needed—not like Palestine and Houston, where the roundhouse and yards moved in 1923. Spring was just a "little fish" in a great sea of railroad travel, and the town simply did not have enough to attract further railroad activity.

And, thus, began the town's downward spiral, hastened by the Great Depression, which weakened the bank and contributed to the enveloping poverty of the area.

Prohibition: "The Rangers Came in and Shot Every Last Bottle!"

To return to Prohibition: Prohibition in Spring is a chapter unto itself. Supposedly, Wunsche Bros. and other Spring saloons were among the last in the area to close at the onset of Prohibition. When the Nineteenth or Prohibition Amendment was enacted in Texas, the law "required saloons located within a certain distance of an army base to be closed a few days earlier than other saloons. Spring was outside of these early closing requirements, but saloons in Houston were closed," states Severance in *Deep Roots, Strong Branches*, a history of the Klein family in North Harris County. Jesse Robinson was a young man working in Wunsche Bros. Jesse's account, recorded some sixty years after that "last night," captures the atmosphere in Spring as legal liquor came to an end.

> The last day that saloons could exist there was a MOB of people from the City of Houston who journeyed to the Town of Spring to "celebrate the sad event," and to obtain that last drink of liquor or bottle of beer. . . .
> Those who gathered for the occasion acted just like the world was coming to an end, as they tried to consume every drop of liquor that was available. Naturally, many of them became very drunk.

> The crowd acted like a funeral had just concluded when the clock struck twelve ending an era . . . .
> The morning after the celebration . . . , in response to an offer by Wunsche Brothers Bar and Saloon to pay five cents for each empty bottle, I spent the day gathering many cases of empty bottles. When I took the cases of empty bottles to the saloon, I was really amazed to see dollar bills and coins in high stacks on the table . . . evidence of the activities of the preceding day and the receipts of the sales.
> This was my first opportunity to see a large number of dollar bills at one time, and the memory and the impression of that experience is still vivid in my mind. . . .

In terms of the closing of Wunsche Bros. Saloon, one may sift through many Prohibition stories, each of which presents a little twist to the scenario of the final hours. In a lively

Supposedly, Wunsche Bros. Saloon was one of the last saloons to close when Prohibition was enacted. The interior of Wunsche Bros. shows the elaborate bar at which crowds of customers were served that last night, a bar still used in Wunsche Bros. today. In describing the last day before Prohibition: "Then," says one patron, "The Texas Rangers came in and shot every last bottle. It was enough to break your heart."

— Courtesy of John Robinson

account, another witness, a Spring citizen, affirms Jesse Robinson's description of that last night when money and liquor ran together as bartenders poured drinks and collected tabs. In this vignette, recorded by Barbara Karkabi, before the evening was over, the desk in the saloon office was stacked high with cash. Then, says the resident of Spring, the night concluded dramatically, "The Texas Rangers came in and shot every last bottle. It was enough to break your heart."

For a brief time, Spring continued as a railroad town, but the loss of the roundhouse—and the loss of legal liquor—brought gradual devastation. The saloons were all shut down; the rooming houses, boarded up. The hospital was torn down; the opera house became a hay barn. With the exception of a couple of little stores, all around settled into decay, a ghost town where once had been a thriving community.

"Moonshine": Risky Business but Business all the Same

The people of Spring could do nothing about the loss of the railroad and loss of financial stability with the coming of the Depression, but the people could do something about the loss of *liquor*—and they did! Maxine Moore writes, "Some say the main thing that saved Spring during this time was bootlegging. Stills were scattered in the woods near Spring and in Montgomery County. They supplied the Houston market."

Avalt Meyer tells of looking across the Spring Creek woods on Sunday morning and seeing many solitary wisps of smoke lifting above the trees, marking the numerous stills at work. Meyer, who, as a boy, hunted the woods near Treaschwig Road, remembers areas in the vicinity as being labeled Hell's Half Acre and Wildcat Prairie, names which suggest the untamed (and illegal) actions of Spring natives during Prohibition! Once, as Avalt, his brother, and friends roamed the area with their guns, looking for game, they heard voices deep in the woods. The Meyer brothers' hunting party tromped toward the noise, thinking they were encountering friends. Instead, they heard a great scrambling and cursing. When the young men reached the clearing from which the voices had echoed, the area was abandoned—all except for the still—a stream of amber elixir still running from the spigot, testifying to another kind of party that had been spoiled by fear that government agents were nearing the illegal brew-factory. Avalt says, "We were half way between Wildcat Prairie and Treschwig Road when we happened on those fellers!"

Although Spring natives touted their moonshine as the best made during Prohibition, certain whiskey-makers were not as skilled as they thought they were, explains Meyer. A number of moonshiners concocted potent raw whiskey (from pond water)—with little time allowed for

Avalt Meyer and his wife Marie farm on Hafer Road, two miles from the busy 1960 highway. Meyer grew up on Aldine Westfield Road where he helped his father with the Meyer family farm. Avalt and his siblings attended the Spring School Annex near their home. With wit and sense of humor, Meyer recalls stories of his youth—events that occurred in or near Spring. Some of Avalt's most vivid memories involve tales of moonshiners. The difference between a moonshiner and a bootlegger, says Avalt is that a moonshiner manufactures liquor, and a bootlegger markets it. In Spring, bootleggers bought moonshine for $1.00 a pint and marketed it for $1.25

of bootlegging in the area. He says, "At one time I think I listed thirty-five bootleggers I knew in the town of Spring." He continues with the tale of how two peddlers of illegal goods pursued their professions:

> There was a fellow used to at 5:00 in the evening when the Forth Worth train would come by . . . would come out of his house all bulged out and go over and crawl up on the engine of the train and he'd unload his bottles. And then when he got off, he'd be back down to normal. . . . And there was a fellow who supposedly had what they called a milk run into Montgomery County, [a county] which was dry. He would deliver whiskey instead of delivering milk, and he would deliver whiskey to various people who would order it. . . .

"curing" or aging. The result was a dangerous drink. Often, the inexperienced operator used a fifty-five gallon *galvanized* tub, instead of a *copper* kettle and fixtures for the still. Alcohol erodes galvanizing, and the tainted liquor from a galvanized still was toxic!

John Robinson comments on the prevalence

Some of Spring's older citizens tell of an aristocratic lady from one of Spring's first families who made a name for herself with her finely brewed whiskey, created within sight of the center of Spring. This same lady served as hostess for raucous parties, attended by townspeople and guests from Houston. On one occasion, the lady, who loved music, invited a talented, young fiddle player and his wife with their infant son to one of her whiskey soirees. The agreement was that the young man would accompany a musical group during the evening's entertainment. The musician played

Spring was not daunted by federal laws! According to one source, "The main thing that saved Spring during this time was bootlegging. Stills were scattered in the woods near Spring and in Montgomery County. They supplied the Houston market."
— Courtesy of John Robinson

and drank—far too much strong home-brew for one unaccustomed to liquor of any kind! In his inebriated condition, the fiddle player could scarcely find his way to his Model-T, much less drive home to Houston. His wife, who *had never* driven a car, was forced to climb behind the steering wheel and navigate family and Ford down the graveled road home to the Houston Heights! Spring water carried a powerful punch!

If revenuers hoped for help from the local law force, they were disappointed. Justice of the Peace, Karl (Charles) Holzwarth was only one example of the lack of support given by Spring officials. Holzwarth's biographer writes:

> While he was Justice of the Peace in Spring, Charles knew who was bootlegging during Prohibition. Whenever he heard that the government men were coming to town, he would pass the word around "Boys, you better move it!"

If the "boys" did not "move it" fast enough, however, the federal lawmen might catch them with the goods. Federal penalties could be rough for a good old boy: time in a federal penitentiary and fines. But *the profits* were worth the risk. Organized crime rings and powerful, unscrupulous individuals believed so, too. During the time of Prohibition, bootlegging was a good business everywhere. But secrecy for any man in the business, the small operator or the big one, was critical.

As late as the 1950's, when Prohibition existed as only a bad dream (yet bootlegging was still a crime), isolated stills remained in operation near Spring. One gentleman regularly made his living in the old-fashioned way, hid his liquor in the hog pen, regularly got caught, and spent a year in jail—over and over again. Others were there, too. A point which shows the Spring conscience in terms of making illegal whiskey: when one of Spring's most prolific moonshiners was preparing for a trip to the penitentiary, his children had to fill out a personal questionnaire for him. When they came to the blank that called for their father's occupation, they knew nothing else to write; they entered in the blank *bootlegger*. Threats of a sentence at the federal prison in Leavenworth, Kansas, did not squelch the moonshiners on Spring Creek!

The Depression: "A Languid Country Town"

Not much more can be said about downtown Spring during the years between 1930 and 1960. The population stabilized at about five hundred, according to road signs. The 1940 census recorded 700 people in the township. The schools had perhaps 250 children in twelve grades and had scarcely enough money to keep the school doors open. One year there was simply not enough money left in the school budget to pay the teachers to the end of their contracts. Superintendent John Winship and his schoolteacher wife Pearl gave up their pay checks so that needy teachers could receive pay.

During the Depression, the federal government sponsored relief projects to help poverty-stricken areas, such as Spring. The government equipped a cannery, located first in a cottage by the bank building and then in the old Salyers store on Midway Street beside the Baptist Church. Local labor had jobs in the cannery, canning vegetables grown by local farmers. During the '30's, Government trucks brought in loads of clothes, shoes, and other items for the poorer people, some of whom lived on dirt floors down Riley Fuzzel Road near Spring Creek. Bayer's sawmill continued to operate and sounded its noon whistle every weekday. Always, the trains ran, but they stopped infrequently, and the train depot operated with a skeleton crew. In the twenty-three Dun and Bradstreet Listings for the Spring area in 1952, *only four* were located in downtown Spring—as opposed to *fourteen* in the 1914 listing. People came into town (which had become a crossroads) on Saturday to buy groceries and feed for livestock; some stayed to drink away their wages at Spring Cafe.

World War II came and went. Spring boys enlisted or were drafted. Some never returned; some returned wounded, physically and mentally. The war was a sad time for Americans, and Spring was not excluded from that grief.

The only telephones in town were located in one of the little grocery stores and at Wunsche Motor Co. on Hwy. 75. The local telephone exchange, the Tomball Telephone Company where Gertie Salyers had worked, left after the roundhouse moved. Finally, in 1957, the

The business section of Spring, Texas, 1950.

— Courtesy of Dora Mobley

Even though the Depression was over, downtown Spring remained a wide spot by the tracks at the end of Spring-Cypress Road. Mobley's Store, 202 Main St., had the only phone in the area and sold Sinclair gasoline from a pump out front.

— Courtesy of Dora Mobley

The interior of Mobley's exemplified the true "country store," with a great mixture of items for sale under one roof. The banners in the back feature the bargains of the week. Showcases hold candy and dry goods. The box in the foreground contains shoes, priced at $1.49 for the pair of your choice. The Coca-Cola case is filled with iced-down drinks of all brands. Dora Mobley stands on the far left, then K. R. Mobley, Tom Avara, Billy Carr, and Will Mobley in the hat at the checkout counter. The Mobley's son Ronnie is down at the right.
— Courtesy of Dora Mobley

Across the street at 119 Main was Mallott's Grocery. This store, too was a place of general merchandise. On the far left is a counter for measuring out piece goods (cloth and oil cloth by the yard). Buckets, wagons, and stoves are a few of the visible items there for purchase. The produce bins are on the side, and the bread rack stands in front of the meat market at the rear of the store. Bill Mallott rests his hand on the "cold drink box." His son Willard stands beside him in a store apron. Evelyn Hillegeist is behind the checkout counter. Bill Mallott bought this store from Hamblin and West after his original shop in the Robinson strip center burned. Feed and hay for livestock were available in both Mobley's and Mallott's grocery stores.
— Courtesy of Dorothy Mallott

GROCERY SPECIALS

ADMIRATION COFFEE	lb. 81c
SNOW DRIFT	3 lbs. 69c
STEW MEAT	lb. 25c
SKINNED HAMS	lb. 49c
A J PANCAKE MIX	1¼ lbs. 19c
DECKER'S OLEO	lb. 18c
BALLARD'S BISCUITS	2 cans 25c
SUGAR	5 lbs. 47c
SLAB BACON	lb. 49c
HOME KILLED CHICKEN HENS	lb. 42c

TALL MILK	2 cans 25c
HAMBURGER	3 lbs. $1.00
HOME MADE SAUSAGE	lb. 49c
PECANS	lb. 39c
RED DELICIOUS APPLES	lb. 17c
CELERY	stalk / 19c
BEWLEY'S FLOUR	25 lbs. $1.79

LEONARD KATENKAMP

Will Prepare Your
INCOME TAXES
at his Home
Beginning January 1, 1956, and
continuing through April 15
Phone SK 7-3296

MALLOTT'S GROCERY

SPRING, TEXAS
SEE OTHER SIDE!

A grocery special sheet from 1956 illustrates the price of groceries at the time.

— Courtesy of David Mallott

Spring had once been a part of the Tomball Telephone Company. When this system moved or closed, the town was left with only two or three phones to use to call anywhere.

— Courtesy of John Robinson

SPRING, TEXAS
TELEPHONE DIRECTORY
AREA CODE 713
SEPTEMBER, 1963

SOUTHWESTERN BELL TELEPHONE COMPANY

Finally, in 1957 the town was equipped with telephones—the S K yline exchange. The illustration is from 1963, but the phone book, a mere pamphlet, retained the same appearance for fifteen years.

town was equipped with telephones (all numbers beginning with the prefix S-K—the SKYLINE exchange!). Such a modern convenience made the area less remote, but, generally, Spring remained a languid, country town with little to attract new businesses and families.

Fires and the Spring Fire Department

After years of loss, another element of progress did bring blessings to Spring: the formation of the Spring Fire Department. From the town's beginning, Spring citizens had learned that pine siding goes up fast, and can certainly go up in smoke—fast. In historical data, numerous references are made to the fires in Spring—some of which may be duplicate reports. According to records, Robinson's strip center first burned in 1917. In a 1973 interview, Willie Wunsche says that in 1918, "fire broke out early one morning in Ol Man Brady's stable and burned out a town block before it could be stopped." Different fires, or one and the same?

The first Spring State Bank burned in one of these fires—or separately. Robinson's buildings burned again in 1941; the school for black children burned in 1951; Immanuel Church burned in '53. All were tragedies, but they at last made the point that people *must* be prepared.

Following the hard lesson of the loss of Immanuel Church, the community rallied. The Spring Volunteer Fire Department was formed in 1954. The Fire Department has its own unique spot in Texas history as a "first." The Spring Volunteer Fire Department was the *first* volunteer fire department in Texas to petition the state legislature for the power to tax the community for money to buy equipment and to finance maintenance. The Spring Department was granted the right to tax and became known as Texas Rural Volunteer Fire Department No. 1.

W. W. Weaver, one of those "charter" firemen, and a former fire chief, remembers the "charter" fire truck as being a second hand vehicle of 1934 vintage. Another early truck was a "1946 G. I. Wheeler," as Weaver calls it. The Department had three stations at first: at Wunsche Motor Co. on Hwy. 75; at Joe Brandt's Garage on Spring-Cypress about half a mile west of town; and at Bayer Lumber Company "in case a train blocked the crossings and a fire truck was needed on the east side of the tracks." In terms of enough trucks to fill the three stations: Weaver says the firemen mainly assembled their own out of parts of other trucks. After all, Weaver notes, they could not afford much on an $800.00 a year budget.

Arthur Bayer, another former fire chief, speaks proudly of the Spring Volunteer Fire Department and its service to the area. Going beyond the line of duty, Spring's Fire Department assisted the Texas Forest Service in fighting fires all over North Harris County and South Montgomery County. On April 6, 1963, Spring Fire Department received the award for Outstanding Achievement in Forest Fire Prevention given by the Texas National Forests. This award is one of the few ever issued to a volunteer fire department in the United States. Bayer proudly displays the certificate designating the award in his office, but Weaver still has the replica of Smokey the Bear that came with the honor!

Above: *The fire department accumulated a variety of fire-fighting equipment as the department grew to serve surrounding subdivisions. The Spring Fire Department now has stations in five suburban areas and provides mutual aid to other area fire departments.*
— Courtesy of W. W. Weaver

Left: *The most poignant scene in all of Spring's history is this photograph showing the 1953 destruction of Immanuel Church, on the corner of Border Street and Spring Cypress. The pastor of the church, Rev. Herman Borne, after singeing his hair and burning his hands as he and Spring neighbors pulled what they could from the fire-filled sanctuary, captured the last minutes of the church on film. The cross blazed against a Sunday evening sky for only a few moments, then crumbled. This fire brought about the chartering of the Spring Fire Department.*

On April 6, 1963, Spring Fire Department received an award for Outstanding Achievement in Forest Fire Prevention from the Texas Forest Service. Such an award is rarely given to small volunteer departments.

— Courtesy of Arthur Bayer

TWO MEN DIE

Gasoline Truck Explodes When Hit By Freight Train

Two men were killed about 9:30 a.m. Saturday when a Missouri Pacific freight train was in a collision with a gasoline tank truck east of Spring in North Harris County.

The dead men were riding in one of the three locomotives which erupted into flames moments after the truck exploded.

Authorities identified the victims as R. E. Hickman, 64, a railroad engineer, of Palestine, and John L. Salmon, 20, a railroad brakeman, from Elkhart.

The driver of the truck, James A. Bower, 24, of Spring, escaped serious injury. Bower jumped out of the truck just before it blew up.

He was taken to Houston Northwest Medical Center Hospital, treated for head cuts and then released.

The truck was carrying 8,000 gallons of gasoline enroute to a Conroe service station, according to George Womack, terminal manager for Mission Petroleum Carriers, Inc., of 8816 Mississippi in Houston. Bower had worked for the company about one month.

The 41-car freight was headed to Houston from Little Rock by way of Palestine, said railroad officials.

Bower told Womack he was westbound on Caroline Street and had stopped at the crossing at Hardy Road before starting across the track. He said he did not see a train. There are no signal lights at the crossing.

The 60-foot truck was almost clear of the crossing when struck by the south-bound train. The flaming locomotive continued down the tracks for about a quarter-mile before coming to a halt near the Main Street crossing.

The blast was heard about seven miles away. Persons on FM 1960 near Champions said the ground moved beneath their feet.

C. K. "Chuck" Reome, who lives in the 26000 block of Hardy near the site of the accident, said, "I heard it but it didn't really register until my wife came in and said a gas truck was on fire here." Reome added, "That boy in the truck went to the house next door and then to our house saying, 'Run for your life.'"

Frank Arp, president of the Spring Volunteer Fire Department, who lives in the area, said he was driving south on Hardy when he heard the explosion.

"I got the repercussion and looked in my rear view mirror and saw a ball of fire and tried to outrun the train to the fire station about two blocks away to get the equipment moving," Arp stated.

R. L. Gilliland, owner of the Spring-Drive In

Grocery at Main Street and Hardy, about three blocks from where the accident occurred, said the front locomotive "was a solid inferno".

Highway patrolmen blocked off several roads in the area in an effort to keep motorists away from the blast site. Several residents of the area voluntarily evacuated their homes.

Flames rose 300 feet in the air. The intense heat hampered efforts by firemen to get close to the blaze. The fire was brought under control about 11 a.m. 12 volunteer fire departments from the area fought the inferno.

The tracks were cleared and ready for rail traffic by Saturday afternoon.

Fire dogged the byways of Spring, even after the formation of the fire department. On October 19, 1974, a collision of a gasoline truck and a Missouri Pacific engine resulted in a fiery explosion and the deaths of the engineer and a railroad brakeman. The wreck occurred at the Caroline St. crossing, and the runaway engine roared through Spring, the burning gasoline truck fused to its front.

— Courtesy of W. W. Weaver

The 1974 collision. It is not an exaggeration to say that in Spring people lived by the train and died by the train. Yes, the railroad created the town, but it took its toll in human sacrifice.

— Courtesy of W. W. Weaver

Since 1954, Spring has had eight capable firemen to lead the Department as chief: they are Earl E. Wunsche, Joe Brandt, Bayer, Frank Arp, Weaver, Jim Barker, Anthony Loscuito, and Alan Langford. Just as the schools have gone beyond the town, so has the fire department. Spring now has stations in five suburban areas and provides mutual aid to other fire departments if a fire breaks out or if another type of disaster requiring assistance occurs.

When W. W. Weaver is questioned about his most outstanding memories of fire-fighting, he immediately recalls a fiery disaster that occurred October 19, 1974. On that day, a gasoline truck carrying eight thousand gallons of gas pulled in front of a southbound Missouri-Pacific train at the Caroline Street crossing. The collision resulted in a fiery explosion and in the deaths of both crewmen on the train; a blazing, runaway train carrying the wrecked fuel truck on its front, barreled through Spring. An awesome sight say all witnesses! Weaver states that the train finally stopped south of the town; the Spring Fire Department extinguished the fire and removed the remains of those on board the train.

Spring Station Road and Expansion on the Houston Highway

During the lean years experienced by the center of downtown Spring, one location did grow and prosper; that location was "the highway," the Houston to Dallas route that crossed Spring-Cypress Road just one mile west of the town itself. In order to get to the highway from Spring, one has to literally make a historical digression.

Of course, in 1903, that road to Houston was nothing like the bright ribbon of super highway that it is today. The Houston road was a rough trail—marking an arduous journey to town for Spring folks. Traveling from the heart of Spring to the main road itself presented a challenge, for there was no legal right of way from Spring to the East Montgomery Road (now I-45) and thence to Houston. On January 28,1903, Carl Wunsche, Robert Robinson, and M.C. Kelly made a "landmark" sale: they described and sold tracts of land to Harris County for purposes of a "Right of Way"—the Spring Station Road—connecting the center of Spring township to East Montgomery Road. Today, if one adhered to the property descriptions in these old deeds, one would most likely find Spring shop owners on Midway sitting on part of the old right of way. Nevertheless, this ancient property sale gave citizens of the then thriving town of Spring a legal path to the main road over which to take their goods to market or to travel for other purposes.

As previously noted, travel to Houston was challenging. Earl Wunsche describes the farmer's journey to market in Houston. He says that in pre-World War I days, the trip to Houston from

Pictured is the first page of File No. 47693, the Deed to Right Of Way for East Montgomery to Spring Station Road. On January 28, 1903, landowners Carl Wunsche, R. L. Robinson, and M. C. Kelly sold to Harris County land for a right of way from the township of Spring to the East Montgomery Road. The right of way gave Spring citizens legal access to the Houston highway.

— Copy courtesy of Arthur Bayer

Spring was a two-day horse and wagon journey on an "old dirt and gravel road known as State 19. Wunsche continues, "We'd take our produce to sell in Houston and spend the night in our wagon in Henke Wagon Yard. . . . It was a one-day trip to Houston and one-day back." A 1916 geographical survey of the Spring area shows the route north from Houston to Montgomery County labeled "Montgomery Road," just as it is on those early deeds specifying a right of way.

In later years, that northern route was improved or replaced to become U.S. Highway 75, the artery which connected Houston to Dallas and points north. On Highway 75 at the Spring-Cypress crossing, several businesses operated and flourished prior to and during World War II. On the southwest side of Spring-Cypress was Reichert's Garage that sold Chevrolets to Spring area people. Wunsche Motor Co., on the northwest corner, sold Ford automobiles to local folks.

Set at the corner of Spring Station Road (Spring-Cypress) and the Houston highway, Wunsche Motor Co. marked the entrance and the exit for the town of Spring. Wunsche Motor Co. had a public telephone booth, served as the over land bus stop, and was an auto repair center. Full-service gas was provided at the round Sinclair pumps.

— Courtesy of Archives of Spring Historical Museum

Wunsche's also sold gasoline and offered auto repairs and servicing. After Reichert's closed, the motor company became the hub of the intersection with a public phone booth located in the lobby of the business to allow a phoneless population to make needed calls. Deputy sheriffs often operated from Wunsche's lobby, locating and catching law offenders from their chosen "office." One deputy who performed his job particularly well was a man of great bulk—perhaps Spring was destined to have larger-than-life lawmen. So heavy was he that his car sagged on the driver's side as he rolled down the road. Weight had not always been an issue in this lawman's life; in his youth he had been a rodeo man, so willowy in appearance that he had earned the nickname of "peavine." The inactivity of his years behind the wheel of a patrol vehicle had added layers of flesh to his once slender frame.

Another building next to Wunsche's at various times housed a doctor's office, a sandwich shop, a liquor store, and a dentist. A grocery and feed store—Bud Dueitt's Spring Cash Grocery—also sat by the road. In the late 1940's after World War II, Cascade Movie Theater—its auditorium, a war-surplus Quonset hut—offered flickering entertainment for Spring and the surrounding area. Just down the

highway, H. M. Russell established Russell Gardens.

Russell Gardens, a nursery specializing in hybrid daylilies, is an important part of Spring's more recent history. Owner of the Gardens, Hugh Russell traced the organization of Russell Gardens to 1927. In the early '50's, Russell moved his nursery to Spring. His first farm was on the southeast side of Highway 75, almost at the Spring-Cypress intersection. As his Gardens prospered and grew, Russell relocated on the west side of Highway 75 at Spring-Stuebner Road. Russell claimed to be "America's largest grower (thirty-eight solid acres)" of daylilies. Year after year, Hugh Russell won major awards from the American Hemerocallis Society for his outstanding work as a grower of daylilies. Russell created exotic daylilies and sold his flowers nationally—and even internationally. One of Russell's most prized responses to his lilies came from Mamie Eisenhower, The White House, Washington, D.C., dated August 28, 1956. Mrs. Eisenhower writes:

Dear Mr. Russell
I am truly delighted with your kindness in sending such a generous quantity of Daylilies for our Gettysburg Farm. I know they will add a great deal of beauty to our grounds, and I understand that they have

Spring's entertainment center after the Second World War was the Cascade Theater just down the highway from Wunsche Motor Company.

— Courtesy of Vassar family

Every month, the Cascade Theater published a movie calendar, detailing the film offerings for the month. Here is the list of films for February 1950. Perhaps you are too young to remember these stellar movies, but you will surely recognize the film star on February 12-13. The feature for those days is The Girl from Jones Beach *starring Ronald Reagan!*

— Courtesy of Willard Mallott

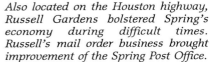

Also located on the Houston highway, Russell Gardens bolstered Spring's economy during difficult times. Russell's mail order business brought improvement of the Spring Post Office.

— Courtesy of Jenny Lee Russell

already been planted where we may see them from our porch—one of our favorite spots!

The President joins me in warmest appreciation for your generous thought of us, and in very best wishes to you.

(signed)
Mamie Dowd Eisenhower

The Gardens provided jobs for struggling Spring people and led to improvement of the Spring Post Office. During the green years of Russell Gardens as Russell mailed his lilies around the world, the magnitude of Russell's postal shipments caused the Spring Post

In early Spring, folks found entertainment in a variety of ways: in the saloons, watching picture shows or traveling entertainers at the opera house, visiting in homes, attending dances and other community events. The Woodmen Hall was frequently the location of such entertainment.

— Courtesy of LuAnne Wunsche

Office to expand from a fourth class post office to a first class post office.

Then the coming of the I-45 freeway to supplant Highway 75 made a business location on the highway even more attractive. In 1960, creation of a shopping center with a supermarket,

a modern pharmacy, a department store, other businesses, and a bank left the downtown center of Old Spring even more forlorn. Just as winter strips away the growth of spring and summer and bares the terrain, the town of Spring withered in the frigid air of poverty and apathy, a partial ghost town where another Spring once bloomed.

Wunsche Bros. Cafe, Hamburgers, and a New Boom

During those years of slow decay, when most of the old buildings vanished, one wooden structure continued to stand in downtown Spring! Even after that night when the Rangers "came in and shot every last bottle," the building that housed Wunsche Bros. Saloon, later Spring Cafe, then Wunsche Bros. again, survived and in a unique way brought back the town. In a *Spring Tribune* article by Bob Veteto, Willie Wunsche leaves the story of the 1902 origin of Wunsche Bros. Saloon. He says:

"It was the first two-story building in Spring. . . . My uncles, Charlie and Dale

Depicted here is another type of entertainment, a family wedding. The wedding party poses on the front porch of Charlie Klein's big house on the Border Street curve. The house, built in 1909, had a verandah that spanned the width of the house and held more than thirty people stretched from one side to the other. This wedding brought together two prominent families in North Harris County, the Kleins and the Goedeckes. The bride is Charlie Klein's daughter Dorothea Bertha Klein and the groom is George Henry Goedecke, Jr.

— Courtesy of Irma Goedecke Wunsche

"THE WOMANLESS WEDDING"
Spring
Community Hall
Friday, August 9th, 8:00 P.M.

--- CAST ---

BRINK'S STORE
General Merchandise

BURKE'S CAFE
Home Cooked Food

F. C. MEYER
Groceries, Westfield

MATHIS FEED STORE
WESTFIELD, TEXAS.

THE BRIDE .... Henry J. Roth
THE GROOM .... Albert Paetzold
THE AUNT .... Edward Haude
THE UNCLE .... R.L. Robinson
THE GRANDMOTHER ... Chas. Klein
THE GRANDFATHER ... Robert J. Haude
THE MOTHER .... Emil Strack
THE FATHER .... Herman Strack
THE TWINS .... Henry Schultz
                    Wilbert Lemm
THE BABY .... Rudolf Lemm
THE NURSE .... Ralph Hanks
TOWN GOSSIP .... Herbert Strack
JILTED SWEET HEART. Chester Strack
FLOWER GIRLS ...... Harry Haude
                    Earl Edrix Wunsche
RING BEARER ...... Awalt Meyer
TRAIN BEARER ...... Richard Meyer
MAID OF HONOR ..... Alvin Wunsche
MINISTER .... Bernard Strack
BEST MAN .... Raymond Strack
BRIDES MAIDS: Fred Strack, Wilbert
    Strack, Alvin Arp, Rudolf Haude,
    Erwin Strack

BENEFIT   Immanuel Evangelical Church
            Spring, Texas.

THANK   YOU

A. E. HILEBRANDT
Garage

A. W. KLEB
Groceries

WINONA THEATER
Tomball, Texas

BRAUTIGAM'S I.G.A STORE
Tomball, Texas.

Left: *The Woodmen Hall was the location for Immanuel Church's 1940 Womanless Wedding. Natalene Sellers recruited the church men and others from the area, including R. L. Robinson and Charlie Klein, to perform in the show. The community loved the program!*
— *Courtesy of Diana Haude*

Another early 1900's photograph shows Dr. O. E. Robertson's son, a very young O. E. Robertson, Jr., posing with his bicycle, a favorite type of recreation at the turn of the twentieth century.
— *Courtesy of Clay Mills*

Wunsche, had put in a sawmill here, but it was wrecked by the Galveston storm. They moved their equipment out in the woods near Klein and then the boiler blew up. . . .

"Old man Charlie had all the lumber he needed. . . . They hauled the lumber to Spring on wagons and my father, William Wunsche Sr., and Ralph Hanks Sr., and Voress Bonin were the carpenters who built the place."

When the saloon opened, the management catered to railroad trade, selling beer at five cents for a tumbler, ten cents for a schooner, and thirty-five cents for a gallon. Rooms over the bar rented for $4.00 a month. The business thrived for almost two decades.

After Prohibition closed the saloon, the structure was used by a several people; one notable landlady was Ada Burke, who called her place the Spring Cafe. Ada was followed by Viola Burke. For twenty-six years, Mrs. Burke operated the Cafe, and the hamburgers she made—eight ounces of juicy, fresh ground beef, cooked just right—became legendary. Louise James in an *Oklahoma* newspaper writes about Spring Cafe: "[In] 1946 the Spring Cafe opened. . . . It soon became famous for its inch-thick hamburgers, onion rings, and chocolate silk pie, drawing regular diners from Houston." After Viola Burke's death, her daughter, Irma Ansley, took over and continued the tradition of fine food that her mother had begun.

Above: *A group of baseball players at Spring School Annex line up for a photograph. Who says a team has to have nine players? The scene is c. 1910.*

Below: *Spring's early town baseball teams remain famous today! The field of play was originally in Spring proper, then moved to an area nearer the Spring Cypress-Houston Highway crossroads. Known as the Spring Boosters in the '20's and '30's, the team celebrated many victories over a variety of opponents including the prisoners' team at the penitentiary in Huntsville. Of course, the Spring team had to travel to Huntsville to play there since the prisoners were not allowed to leave the prison.*

— Courtesy of August Wunsche

Truitt Ferguson   Willie Balke   August Strelau   Dewey Moser   Joe Monroe   L. T. Peveteaux

Lester Larsen   Willie Klein   Phelmo Burke   Eugene Robinson   Earl Wunsche   H. Peveteaux

In 1980, Barbara Karkabi interviewed Irma Ansley and recorded her findings in an article entitled "Spring Cafe claims the best food and slowest service—anywhere." Karkabi notes that once a tourist wrote to Mrs. Ansley from Paris, France: "'The Spring Cafe and the Eiffel Tower were built approximately at the same period, but the hamburgers are still better in Spring!'" In the guest book that Mrs. Ansley kept, the "entries read like a travelogue. The 50 states are all represented as well as faraway points like Australia, Hong Kong, Europe, and the Middle

Another of Spring's teams pauses for pictures on the baseball field behind Wunsche Motor Company in about 1929. Back, left to right: Clarence Kreinhop, Frank Westbrook, Van Johnson, Watson Tomlinson, Albert Kaiser, George Glameyer, Eddie Kaiser. Front left to right: Hugo Kaiser, Shorty Yocum, Julius Klein (known as Skeet) Henry Kreinhop, Laurence Doerre, Bill Kreinhop. Thanks to August Wunsche for identifying these players. Spring's team was spirited, on and off the field. Avalt Meyer tells a story about what may have been this very team of Spring players. The team traveled to Fairbanks, Texas, to play. There they were outscored during the game and also soundly whipped in a fist fight afterward. Always a crew to repay in like manner, the Spring boys waited for Fairbanks to come to Spring to play in a return game. Sometime during the visit, a fight between players again occurred—in Reichert's Garage across the street from the field. This time, the Spring boys, amidst the automobiles in the garage, soundly defeated the Fairbanks opponents, and left one member of the Fairbanks team sitting dazed and almost unconscious behind the wheel of a Chevrolet car, propped up as though he were about to drive away.

— Courtesy of LuAnne Wunsche Schultz

East." Karkabi quotes Mrs. Ansley: " 'I've even heard tell that there is a picture of the Cafe hanging in the Hilton Hotel in Cairo, Egypt. But I don't know how we'd ever find that out for sure.' "

Only one problem existed with the hamburgers at the Spring Cafe, and that problem was really with the cook, not the food. *Service was notoriously slow.* Customers were known to wait as long as three hours to be served. On Saturday afternoons, the line to get in Spring Cafe could stretch around the block. Enterprising entrepreneurs, noting lines of people with money and no place to spend it, created specialty shops nearby, anxious to "grab the attention of restaurant guests." The first of these shopkeepers was Sharon Blakeman, who rented the old brick drugstore on Midway, decorated the building, stocked it with antiques and novelties, and called it "The Checkered Churn." The efforts were contagious, and today Old Town Spring is another kind of boomtown, containing "170 specialty shops, galleries, restaurants, and museums." Spring attracts a world class clientele—a new town created from the selling power of a hamburger!

The Spring Cafe was to receive its just reward for endurance, a medal for longevity and service. In 1984, the building was restored to its original condition and given its original name

Look at those white tailed deer, most likely from the Spring Creek bottom! This scene from the 30's shows the spoils of the deer hunt, deer carcasses hanging on the front of Klein's Red and White Grocery. The grocery store first belonged to R. L. Robinson; Alvin and Alex Klein leased the store from Robinson in 1922 until the late '30's. At the Red & White Grocery, the Klein brothers sold funeral caskets as well as groceries and dry goods, thus, the very first beginnings of Klein Funeral Home, now in Tomball. Later occupants of stores at this site were Will Mobley and then Vernon and Henry (Buddy) Doering.

Back to the deer: In those days, deer hunters did not have to travel far to have a good hunt. Woods in the area held enough game for all. Alec Klein, in the bow tie, was probably not one of the hunters.

— Courtesy of John Robinson

Perhaps this form of recreation could be called "the poor man's deer hunt." Farm men and boys gathered and spent the night using their shotguns to rid the local barns of rat infestation. Here, the young men are assembled after a particularly good night of "rat killing." Anxious to show their quarry, the hunters have loaded their lines and have even more rats on the ground. The men are from left to right: Erwin Kleb, Henry Treichel, Otto (Kelly) Theiss, Milton Klek, Christian Strack, Otto Krahn, and Emil Theiss. The youngest hunter, twelve year old Andrew Kleb, is not posing for the camera because he was wounded in the fray. When an older hunter used a knife to spear one of the dead animals, young Andrew's hand got in the way, and he was speared by his fellow rat killer. Andrew is in the house getting first aid!

— Courtesy of Marjorie Meier

The original Wunsche Bros. Saloon, the first two-story building in Spring, was built by Charlie and Dell Wunsche in 1902. This is one of those buildings that we wish could talk! What tales it could tell. Of fun inside and fights inside and out. Of the final night before Prohibition when Wunsche Bros. was the last saloon to close in North Harris County. Of raucous nights and sleepy days, booze, good food, and fine fellowship. Where does the list stop when a house has witnessed one hundred years of living?

— Courtesy of Wunsche archives

While the men participated in less-than-genteel activities, the ladies put on their hats and went to town—or to church. Members of the Ladies Aid of Immanuel Church pose in front of the church as the women join in commemorating the church's Thirtieth Anniversary in 1946. Here is a partial (and speculative) list of the group: Alice Hanks Lemm is in the checked dress on the left; next to her is Rosa (Mrs. Charles) Holzwarth; Ella Klein Doering or Frieda Strack is the lady clutching her purse by Rosa. In the center in a dark dress and hat is Alma Lemm (Bode); Meta Klein Strack has her bag tucked under her arm; Jewel Arp Faetche is the last lady on the front row. Dorothy Mallott is to Jewel's left in black hat and dress. Marie Paetzold, bare-headed, stands to Mallott's right, and the short woman by Marie with white on her hat is Dora Schultz Lemm. Mrs. R. L. Robinson may be the lady in the large black hat at the far back behind Dora Lemm. The first Immanuel sanctuary serves as the backdrop for the group.

— Courtesy of Immanuel Church archives

The Spring Cafe, housed in the old Wunsche Bros. building, did not have much going for it—except the best hamburgers in North Harris County, and the slowest service in the county. The hamburger kept the cafe, the building, and later, the town, alive.

— Courtesy of Spring Historical Museum

of Wunsche Bros. Cafe and Saloon. The restoration earned Wunsche Bros. a place in the Texas Register of Historic Places. With much festivity, and in the company of Wunsches who were descendants of the original builders Charlie and Dell Wunsche, plus area residents and guests, the Harris County Historical Commission held dedication ceremonies for the historical site. The great medallion and plaque on the front of the building tell the story of Spring's oldest commercial building that is still standing.

Historical Structures in Spring

Although many of the buildings that contain shops in Old Spring have been moved in or have been newly constructed on-site to follow the late Victorian, early twentieth-century motif of the town, many other structures, such as Wunsche Bros., the old brick drug store just down Midway, and the bank building next door to the drug store, survive from Spring's 1900 boom. The Robinson houses described earlier and certain other bungalows that were original Spring dwellings have been converted to shops. The remodeled and restructured McLachlan home-

Hotel-saloon in Spring celebrates its designation as historic landmark

Sam C. Pierson Jr. / Chronicle

Built in 1902 by one of Spring's earliest families, the Wunsche Bros. Cafe & Saloon, later known as The Spring Cafe, was recently designated by the state of Texas as a significant historical structure, typical of the German railroad settlement at the turn of the century. The building is Spring's oldest existing commercial building on its original site. Using most of the original materials, the building was restored to its original condition by local residents and co-owners Scott Mitchell and Brenda Greene, earning its place in the Texas Register of Historic Places. The Harris County Historical Commission held dedication ceremonies recently for the establishment in Old Town Spring during the annual Heritage Holidays. Mitchell shakes hands, above, with Willie Wunsche, 95, the oldest descendent of Carl and Jane Wunsche, who had owned and operated the hotel and saloon as a family business. Many area residents, some in period costume, left, attended the unveiling of a special marker at the front door. The dedication followed a parade celebrating Heritage Holidays.

The restored Wunsche Bros. Cafe and Saloon rated a place in the Texas Register of Historic Places. Dedication ceremonies occurred on October 17, 1984, a festive day in Old Town Spring. Uncle Willie Wunsche rejoiced with the new owners of Wunsche Bros.

— Courtesy of *Houston Chronicle*

Today, as one approaches Spring on Hardy Street from the north, Wunsche Bros. sits imposingly ruling the town, Of the five two-story hotels/boarding houses originally in Spring, only Wunsche Bros. remains. Note the commemorative plaque and medallion on the lower verandah.

On a busy day in Old Town Spring, Wunsche Bros. has to lift its head high to be seen above the automobiles crowding the streets.

stead, now a bed and breakfast on Hardy Street; the stately Henry-Bayer family home on Aldine-Westfield Rd.; the George Goedecke home, also restructured, on Spring Stuebner; the redecorated house on Main Street called Whitehall—are examples of early dwellings that still serve as living quarters for Spring folk.

Three original residences in Spring deserve special treatment because of their particular circumstances: these three are the aforementioned Whitehall, the Thurman home on Elm Street and the Wilson-Mallott House located at the end of Mallott Road.

THE CLINE-HARPER HOUSE (WHITEHALL)

Since this imposing two-story structure has been turned over, in part, to specialty shops as Robinson's cottages have, Whitehall has been absorbed into the commerce of Old Town Spring. Yet no study of the town would be complete without a comment about Whitehall since the striking Victorian home with added decor has become a symbol for the town. The house has been featured on the cover of books about the area and on the front of at least one year's telephone book for the North Harris County area.

Located on the corner of Keith Street and Main, the house was reputedly created in 1897

The Cline-Harper House, or Whitehall, as it appeared in years before statuary and decorations were added.

by sawmill owner Cline for the Harper family. Hence, the building is often referred to as the Cline-Harper House. The house has had many notable occupants and purposes over the years. Alex Klein (of Klein Funeral Home and Klein Grocery Store in Tomball) and his family resided here in the '20's and '30's, says Diana Severance in her history of the Klein family. At first, the Kleins shared the home with a Goe-

decke family, the Kleins living upstairs and the Goedeckes, downstairs. The Klein children, perhaps six of them, were born in an upstairs bedroom of this house.

Alex and his brother George Klein, with help from various members of their family, operated the Red and White Grocery Store on Main Street. Alex Klein worked himself into the funeral business by selling caskets for the deceased in Spring. Eventually, he made funeral arrangements in addition to sale of caskets, and he became a licensed funeral director. Hence, the Klein Funeral Homes of Tomball germinated here in a corner of Spring. Some sources say Alex worked out of his home on Main for a while before the Kleins bought the old Townsend Grocery and used the ground floor of the store to display sample coffins.

Another notable resident of Whitehall was John Winship, long-time superintendent of Spring Independent School District. Winship and his family lived in the house in the '40's and '50's.

A most vivid sight, the house now has an ornamental fence, a gazebo, statuary, a garden, and a greenhouse—a true photographer's subject. Tours are available as is a brochure outlining other possible events in the building's history.

THE THURMAN HOME

Completed in 1921, the Thurman home

The Thurman home, completed in 1921, with historic marker on the front porch. The house earned the marker because only one family, the Thurman family, has occupied the house in the seventy-nine years since it was built.

has earned a historical marker from the State of Texas because in those eighty years since the house was built, only one family has occupied the 26811 Elm St. residence—the family of W. E. Thurman. Historically, the Thurman home is "all-Spring." Thurman hired Spring contractor J. W. Salyers to erect the house and financed the building venture through Spring State Bank, later going to the bank periodically with his daughter Ila to make payments on the note. Thurman and his wife Alma Klein Thurman reared their children in the house; the youngest, Kenneth, was born there. Some years after her husband had been killed in a tragic accident, Alma Thurman experienced her last illness in the family home. After the elder Thurman's death, daughter Ila occupied the one-story, white structure until her own demise.

Even though Ila Yvonne (I.Y.) Thurman remodeled the interior and put aluminum siding on the exterior, she kept many of the original features of the house. With the exception of a modification of the porch, the shape of the front of the house is the same. The front columns are the original ones—made from heart of pine. Inside, the first soft pine floors are still in use as is a walnut window seat that Salyers built. Also the heating stove standing in the dining area is the one used by the Thurman family over the years.

The Thurman home—an existing record of one family's growth—is tied historically to certain features in the development of old Spring.

THE WILSON-MALLOTT HOUSE

Another family home, the Wilson-Mallott House has no historical marker, although perhaps it should. Spring's most elegant and well-preserved house, dating from c. 1898, cannot be found on traveled streets as these other buildings are. This Victorian farm house stands just half a mile from Old Town Spring at the end of Mallott Road, hidden by a cover of pecan trees and other sheltering vegetation. Built by Frances Wunsche Wilson—granddaughter of German pioneer settler, Carl Wunsche—and her husband James Wilson, a retired railroad man, the two story structure is "in a style that had been popular since the mid 1800's with a large

porch and high pitched roof," says David Mallott. The house includes an assortment of bay window areas, gingerbread trim, and turned wood for decoration. The cypress siding on the house is the original; not one of the first boards has ever required replacement!

A picture of the house taken soon after it was built reveals how imposing the white house must have been, standing on open prairie at the time, clearly visible from most points on the Spring Station Road. August Wunsche tells of seeing the house from the road when he was a small boy, riding in a buggy to town with his mother, or walking on his way to school. At the time, Woodrow Wilson was President of the United States, embroiled in a spate of politics prior to, and during, World War I. Wunsche says that each day at home he heard his parents talking about Mr. Wilson's actions and decisions in the *White House*. Knowing that a Wilson (who was one of his relatives) lived in the big, *white house* in Spring, young August confused the two, coming to believe that Matters of State were being solved in remote Spring and that each day on his trip to town he was seeing *THE White House*. August's mother finally explained the dif-

Built by James and Frances Wilson in the late 1800's, the Wilson-Mallott house, with surrounding barns and sheds, originally composed a "model" farm.

Frances Wunsche Wilson loved to entertain in the setting of her new home. In 1903, Frances' niece Bridget Kelly married in this house. Frances and husband James Wilson feted the newlyweds afterward. Here is an attempt to identify the group at the wedding party for those who cherish history. The listing has been created, in part, by Alvin Wunsche and John Robinson, although both were uncertain in some instances. Rear row, left to right: Grandma Wunsche; Mary Kelly; Katie Harless; Dell Wunsche; the bride Bridget Estelle Kelly Walton; the groom Edward B. Walton; perhaps Bridget's father, Mike Kelly; an unnamed lady; Allie Wunsche; another unnamed lady; Grandma Sellers; Mrs. Julia Sellers Robinson; R. L. Robinson. Front row, left to right: Urilda Kothman; O. M. Dullos (or Charlie Wunsche); John Salyers; Mrs. Salyers; unnamed lady; James Wilson, the host; Frances Wilson; William Wunsche; Clementine Hargrave; Sophronia Wunsche, William's wife; unnamed lady; Grandpa Sellers, Bud Wunsche; Allie Bender or John Miller. William and Sophronia's little ones sit in front: Pearl, Willie, Earl, and James.

ferences in the two *white houses,* but his childish confusion remains a family joke to this day.

Earl Wunsche commented about the home of his aunt, Francis Wilson: "The place was a showplace when it was first built." Earl believed that the lumber of the house did not come from Wunsche Mill as Wunsche Bros. did. He says that James Wilson, a railroad bridge foreman, used his retirement money for the house and farm buildings. The Wilsons planned the house, had the lumber shipped in, and used out-of-town carpenters for the construction.

Interior features of the Wilson home are lavish for a farm house. The living room, with a twelve foot ceiling, has a fireplace of glazed tile with a hand-carved wood mantle; the wainscoting in the hallway is beaded and stained a rich mahogany as are the twelve-inch baseboards throughout the house. All the doors, interior

and exterior, are topped with working transoms. The exterior doors have stained glass panels. The stair case is resplendent with wood work and contains an elegant Newell post and a stair rail supported with turned mahogany spools. The date of 1898 is only a guess, but Willie Wunsche could remember spending the night of the famous 1900 Galveston storm in the house, which was completed at that time. Newspapers from 1899 and 1900 were used as padding for the original carpeting on the stairs.

Willard and Dorothy Mallott purchased the house in 1936 as part of a forty-acre farm for which they paid $4,210.00. Besides the house and land, the purchase included a complete array of farming equipment and a wind mill; chicken house; triple garage; two-story buggy shed; smoke house; and hay barn containing a spacious loft, stalls, pens, and feed rooms.

Maintained and preserved over the years, the Wilson-Mallott House is one of the landmarks of North Harris County. The integrity of the original house has been maintained, making it a significant part of Spring's history.

The symbol of Old Town Spring, Whitehall is on Main at Keith Street. Delightful stories circulate about this imposing old house which was created in 1897 by sawmill owner Cline for the Harper family.

The remodeled and restructured McLachlan homestead is now a bed and breakfast on Hardy Street. This homestead has remained in the McLachlan family since 1862. In 1910, Charles McLachlan, who later became Superintendent of the Spring Independent School District, remodeled the original house, using lumber from the area that is now The Woodlands. Jim and Jocelyn (McLachlan) Clairmonte again remodeled the family home in 1988, expanding the original six hundred square feet to almost three thousand, additions being used to accommodate guests. Exquisitely furnished with family pieces and antiques, Jim and Jocelyn have retained the ambiance of an elegant, late nineteenth century home, yet created a place of great comfort for visitors and patrons. This loving and exact replication of detail from earlier days makes McLachlan Farm an important historical site in Spring.

The Henry-Bayer home (1914) on Aldine-Westfield Road with a magnificent old oak in the front yard deviates from the late Victorian architecture of the town with its classic pillars and flat front. The facade suggests a modified Greek Revival style, perhaps by an architect not common to the Spring area.

Cemeteries

A town still stands on, and around, the "Robinson Addition" to Spring. Enough of the old structures survive for those remaining behind to say "Spring is still here." A semblance of Spring survives in the midst of shops and tourists who come for the day. But where are the old pioneers: the ones who experienced the Spring of an earlier day? Those folks, for the most part, rest in the cemeteries in or near the town, cemeteries as old as the town. Just as churches and schools must be pared down to get to what was (is) truly Spring—so must a history be selective of the cemeteries that truly served the town. Five places of rest rank as the most significant to Spring history: Budde Cemetery just off Louetta Road; the tiny Wunsche Family Cemetery, in a sheltered nook by I-45; St. Matthew's Cemetery in Westfield; Spring Cemetery on Aldine-Westfield Road near the exposed foundation of the old Spring School; and Peaceful Rest Cemetery on East Hardy, the burial ground used by the black families of Spring. Although comprehensive studies have been made of Texas cemeteries, such as Trevia Beverly's *At Rest: A Historical Directory of Harris County, Texas, Cemeteries,* documentation of these isolated, sometimes neglected, burial spots is difficult to find.

Many of the turn-of-the-twentieth century buildings, such as the Charlie Klein house, built in 1909 and located behind Immanuel Church, just off Border Street, have fallen down or have been torn down. Charlie Klein, an important figure in the development of Spring, was a mail carrier in Spring for thirty years; he was a Spring constable and justice of the peace and a charter member of Immanuel Church; and he was one of the original trustees of Spring I.S.D. What a shame that his great house could not have been preserved in his memory.

— Courtesy of Irma Wunsche

However, the Mallotts soon found they were not farmers, but merchants instead. They opened a small grocery store on Main Street, and that business remained their livelihood. The Mallott name was on a business in downtown Spring for fifty-nine years—Mallott's Grocery Store, Mallott's I.G.A. Store, Mallott's Hardware and Variety, Mallott's Western Wear. Today, most of the out-buildings of the farm are gone, but the Mallotts kept the house in first-class condition. Their son Willard, Jr., also lived here and did much to restore and maintain the house; now Willard Mallott's children and grandchildren live here. Four generations of Mallotts have cherished this old house and called it home.

BUDDE CEMETERY

Budde Cemetery, often referred to as the Budde-Holzwarth Cemetery, is out of Spring proper, at the end of Budde Cemetery Road. The cemetery land, originally a corner of the Budde property, was designated for use as a "family and friends" cemetery. Somewhere along the way, one of those German property feuds encompassed the cemetery, and for years a fence divided the plot into two parts: one group of families buried on one side and another group on the other. The feud may have stemmed from a desire on the part of some of the members of Immanuel Church to turn the cemetery into a church cemetery. Many of the founders of Immanuel Church and their families are buried here along with Carl Wunsche and his descendants. In January 1914, Charles and Rosa

Budde Cemetery, once alone in a corner of the Budde property, is now surrounded by subdivisions. Budde has served as a burial spot for 150 years.

Holtzwarth deeded the cemetery plot to "Trustees appointed for the . . . Budde Cemetery ground." The deed set aside any threat that the cemetery might become a private burial spot, not open for those for whom it was intended.

Today, an active Budde Cemetery Association monitors the condition and use of the area. The graves date from the mid-1800's, indicating the locale has served as burial spot for almost 150 years. The stone markers are provocative and make a study themselves. A Tautenhahn family tombstone in the form of a four-sided obelisk records the deaths of five members of the same family: *Hier Ruhet Carl Tautenhahn, Geb Ap 1827 Gest den 27 Aug 1870 und desen Ehefrau Fredericke Geb Jan 20 1829 Gest dem 17 Aug 1870* is engraved on one side of the stone ("Here lies husband and wife"); on another side, *und deren Tochter Hedwig Geboren in Sachsen Ruhet Hier in Frieden* (their daughter); the deaths of two other Tautenhahn children are recorded on the monument. This stone and others in this aged cemetery say much to the visitor about the time period of the deceased, about family unity, and about tragic infant mortality.

WUNSCHE FAMILY CEMETERY

The smallest, and yet the most well-known of Spring's cemeteries, is Wunsche Family Cemetery. The little plot has received notoriety because of its locale in a sheltered and preserved niche just adjacent to the I-45 freeway one block south of Cypresswood Drive. The freeway was designed and built so as not to disturb the cemetery. The Wunsches buried there are relatives of the Carl Wunsche family, but some spell their names "Wuensche," a fact which may be observed on certain of the tombstones. Twenty marked graves are in the plot, but soil indentions indicate other graves may be there, unmarked. The oldest grave is of a child, M. O. Lorenz Wunsche, *"Geb. 3, Dec 1879 and Gest. 25, Sept 1885."* The inscription on this headstone, and on others, is in German script. It reads *"Denn seine Seeke gesullt Gott darum lilel er mit ihm aus* [sic]." (translated: "Because his soul pleases God, Therefore He hastens with him out of this life.") The youngest to be buried in Wunsche Family Cemetery is the infant son of Julia and Alvin Wunsche, interred in 1941. Buried most recently is Juliane O. Wuensche whose life spanned from 1876 to 1959.

The oldest grave in the Wunsche Family Cemetery is September 1885. The Cemetery is sheltered by the I-45 freeway and gets attention because of its prominent location.

ST. MATTHEW'S CEMETERY

St. Matthew's Lutheran Church Cemetery rests behind St. Matthew's on Meyer Road. The cemetery has over 150 grave sites. Begun in 1911, the cemetery has mainly served settlers who were German farmers—and their descendants. Because of restorations, spearheaded by Charles Meyer, whose family is buried in the cemetery, the cemetery is fenced, has two iron archways, and statuary, including a Christ the Good Shepherd statue. Now, a concrete circular drive runs into the cemetery. The spot has

St. Matthews Church Cemetery is lovingly tended. A wrought-iron fence and statuary add to the pleasant setting.

become so beautiful and so dear to the congregation of St. Matthew's that "[the] church now holds yearly Easter Sunday sunrise services in the refurbished cemetery." An account by Steven Pittman details the extent of St. Matthew's restoration.

One of the earliest graves in the cemetery is the resting place of Paul F. Kaiser, who lived from April 30, 1896, to November 9, 1918. Paul was killed in France during World War I. Another young one buried there is Janice Delon Cade, placed beneath a heart shaped pink granite marker. Janice, who lived from 1953 to 1973, is "At Rest With Jesus." Names in the cemetery are like German roll-call: Hafer, Hildebrandt, Doberschutz, Schulz, Schindewolf, Ehrhardt, Beckendorf, Mittelstedt, Musgrove—the list goes on.

Certain rules must be followed if one is to be buried in this cemetery. Plots are reserved for St. Matthew's church members or those who were "communicant members of St. Matthew's for at least five years. Funeral services must be performed by a Lutheran church Missouri Synod pastor." Charles Meyer sees the cemetery as a history lesson in itself, the graves causing the living to remember and revere the dead.

SPRING CEMETERY

Spring Cemetery, the town burial site, was established on land donated by the Sellers family for a church, [school], and burial ground. J. C. Sellers deeded the cemetery property originally to the Methodist Church, one of the denominations that met in the adjacent church building called the Union Church. In record, that first Methodist Church still owns the cemetery property located at 26206 Aldine-Westfield Road.

The graves in the cemetery present a profile of the town. Names of old Spring families such as Bonds, Baker, Herren, Haskins, and Toomer are delineated on the grave markers. The earliest discernible date is 1910 on the grave of Frank Leroy Lovins, and the most recent burial seems to be 1969. The graves of veterans from earlier wars, including a Civil War veteran, George C. Baker, are there. A Woodmen of the World, Ralph E. Fritz (1912) with the accompanying Woodmen tree trunk used as a gravestone, is

Overgrown, with monuments damaged by vandals, the Spring Cemetery has been long neglected. The designation of the spot as a historical site should bring maintenance and restoration to the little town cemetery with graves dating from 1910.

buried in the cemetery. One community headstone marks the graves of mother and daughter, placed side by side. Testifying to the fickle nature of life, headstones for infants and the aged are present there together.

A group of North Harris College Honors students in 1999 surveyed the cemetery and found forty-seven identifiable grave sites although many other graves are most likely unmarked or the markings have deteriorated with time. In 2000, Spring Cemetery was designated as a Texas Historic Landmark with an appropriate marker denoting the graveyard's historical ranking.

PEACEFUL REST CEMETERY

On what is one of the loveliest of cemetery sites, Spring's Peaceful Rest Cemetery is located on East Hardy Street within sight of the Hardy Tollway. The three and four-tenths acres, partly wooded, is situated on a knoll and slopes down toward Spring Creek. Like the Spring Cemetery, Peaceful Rest is on land deeded to the commu-

nity by J.C. Sellers. On July 31, 1923, Sellers put pen to paper and directed that "I, J. C. Sellers of the County of Harris State of Texas for and in consideration of the sum of $1.00 to me paid by Colored People of the Town of Spring in Harris County donated for a Cemetery, or Grave Yard." The deed indicates that this plot is part of the A. G. Holland survey, "the same being made once for an orphan home for the colored children but abandoned."

All burial spots in this cemetery are free with only the request from the cemetery committee for a donation for upkeep. In the cemetery, many graves are unmarked, and some of the marked graves are indistinguishable, the older stones being of poor quality and worn smooth by the weather. These old markers, plus handmade markers with names roughed in, illustrate the poverty some of the African-Americans in the community faced. Later monuments are more elegant and ornate than older ones, reflecting a more prosperous lifestyle. Names like Barnet, Lee, Williams, Franklin, King, Bradie, Mays, Sayles, Holland, Phillips, and Booker are examples of long-time Spring citizens buried in Peaceful Rest Cemetery.

Spring's Peaceful Rest Cemetery is located in a lovely spot on a knoll sloping down to Spring Creek. Burial spots in this cemetery are free. Plans are to maintain and restore this historic site.

Spring: Through the Seasons— Blooming Again

Most will agree that generally small towns in urban America did not fare well in the face of progress. Those agrarian concerns, which had called for manual labor and kept the "boys down on the farm," were diminished by twentieth century changes. Manufacturing, commercialism, and technology brought centralization in big cities and sucked the backroads dry of a hard-working population looking for an easier life. The town of Spring bloomed early, then wilted as the farms became outdated, and the rails slighted the town. But Spring, unlike so many of its Texas counterparts, did not disappear, even when lifestyles faltered and faded.

What really kept the town going? The answer is inherent in the *story* of the town. Spring was like that Western town of Tombstone, "too tough to die." To say that Spring was a town of "proud fighters" is no exaggeration. Look back at their stories, and you find Spring's lifeblood flowing through steely patrons. The remaining descendants of that band of Germans, railroad workers, and sawmill people that melded during the first fifty years of the twentieth century resulted in a numerically thin, but tough breed that stuck with the town during the hard times. Tenacity was their hallmark, and they were not about to leave and move to higher ground!

Their loyal attitude was reflected in the comment of one of the town's *grand dames*, a comment made when Spring was in its lowest state. The lofty lady said: "I'd move to Houston if I could live where I want to there. In West University Place or River Oaks. Since I can't begin to afford those places, I'll just stay right here in good ol' Spring and pretend to make my own River Oaks!"

Today, most of that old, independent breed is gone, replaced by stores, vendors, and their world-class customers, who shop over the bones of old Spring and bask in the mythical "charm, warmth, and ambiance of down-home memories."

In terms of what Spring was, and what Spring is, perhaps all that is left of the original town is a memory, "*a casual* history." Yet that thought is much too negative! It is more pleasant to think that Spring is a trade community continuing to evolve. Perhaps, the shopping boom today, built on the selling power of a hamburger, is a continuing *spring,* a renewal of trade in an on-going development of this tiny trade town north of Houston, a town that can trace its legacy to Indians and German settlers trading fish for bread, to farm trade on the Houston market, to a home for busy iron horses and saw mills, to a center for moonshine, moonshine so delicious as to bring its own plethora of trade!

Mrs. Betty John Avara coordinates the volunteers who staff the Spring Historical Museum, a museum designed to preserve the history and lifestyles of early Spring people. Museum volunteers work tirelessly to tell the Spring story!

This pen and ink, aerial drawing of Old Town Spring, the shopping village, allows one to see the new blooming of Spring, a town that survived through the seasons.

Significant Dates in the Development of the Community of Spring, Texas

1840 . . . . A recorded population of 153 people, numbers fed by an influx of German immigrants who came into the area.

1871 . . . . A railroad line laid through Spring by the Houston and Great Northern Railroad Company to run from Houston, north to the Red River.

1873 . . . . Creation of Spring. The railroad filed a subdivision plat creating the Town of Spring, a twenty-block village near the current business section of Old Town Spring (later reduced to sixteen blocks).

1889 . . . . Formation of the first lumber mill. The densely wooded land prompted many mills in the area during these early years.

1890 . . . . Record of the first school, a wood-frame, one-room structure about a mile south of Spring.

1900 . . . . Spring's recognition as a major railroad switch yard. When the Fort Worth line was constructed right in the middle of town to intersect with the Great Northern Line, Spring became an established railroad junction, boasting a roundhouse and, later, fourteen track yards.

1902 . . . . Creation of Robinson Subdivision —the present location of Old Town Spring.

1902 . . . . Spring's building boom, brought on by railroad traffic. Saloons— such as Wunsche Bros.—hotels, an opera house, a hospital, and other recreational and commercial structures sprang up overnight! For a short time,

Spring was growing as fast as its mighty neighbor, Houston!

1907 . . . . Establishment of Spring Independent School District.

1910 . . . . Chartering of Spring State Bank— $10,000 in capital, 100 shares of stock. The population of Spring was 1200 folks of a lively and diverse nature.

1919-1933 . . . . Prohibition. The saloons closed!

1923 . . . . Move of the railroad roundhouse (then Missouri Pacific) to Houston.

1927 . . . . Establishment of Bayer Excelsior Mill. Gus Bayer later opened Bayer Lumber Co.

1929-1933 . . . . The Great Depression. As in all of the United States, Spring suffered through an era of great poverty.

1934 . . . . Merger of Spring State Bank with Guaranty Bond State Bank of Tomball.

1935 . . . . Consolidation of Rural School District No. 8 into Spring Independent School District.

1939 . . . . Opening of Carl Wunsche School, as a senior high school, at its present location

1940-1963 . . . . Commerce in small businesses (Russell Gardens, Bayer Lumber Co., Cascade Theater, and others).

1950 . . . . A recorded population of 500 people. Just as so many other small Texas towns, Spring was in a state of decline.

1960 . . . . Construction of a shopping center and bank at I-45 and Spring-Cypress. The move from the railroad crossing to I-45, one mile west, further decimated the original center of Spring.

1979 . . . . Beginning of restoration of Spring with the creation of novelty and specialty shops in some of the original town structures.

1984 . . . . Recognition for Wunsche Bros. Cafe and Saloon as a Texas historical landmark. Wunsche Bros. is Spring's oldest existing commercial building on its original site.

1984 to Present Development and growth of Old Town Spring as a shopping village and recreational area.

Sources

"As recalled by W. T. Wunsche: Early history of Spring community is a quiet one." *The North Harris County News.* Wednesday, July 18, 1973. N. pag.

Avara, Betty John. Personal Interview. Spring, TX. November 9, 2000.

Bayer, Arthur. Personal Interview. Spring, TX, July 6, 1992; February 21, 2000; October 23, 2000.

Benefield, Naomi. Telephone Interview. April 21, 2000.

Benjamin F. Clark. Biographical Sketch. Spring Independent School District archives.

Beverly, Trevia Wooster, comp. *At Rest: A Historical Directory of Harris County, Texas, Cemeteries (1822-1992).* Houston: Texas Publications & Research, 1993.

Binford, T. A. Sheriff. Letter to Mr. H. D. Brown, Cashier of Spring State Bank. January 7, 1933. Spring Historical Museum archives.

"A Brief History." Spring Independent School District archives. N. dat.

Campbell, Thomas N. "Akokisa Indians." *The Handbook of Texas Online.* February 15, 1999. (http//www..tsna. utexas. edu/handbook/online/articles/view/AAeqr 1/ .html).

Clairmonte, Joycelyn. Personal Interview. Spring, TX, October 1995; February 2000.

Clark, B. F. "The History of Southwell, the Spring School for Black Students." N. dat. Spring Independent School District archives.

Clark, B. F. Personal Interview. Spring, TX. June 13, 2000.

"Constable Harless Dead from Wound." *Houston Chronicle.* Friday, April 16, 1915:3.

Deed of Right of Way for East Montgomery to Spring Station Road (copy). March 17, 1903.

Deed of Sale of Budde Cemetery Ground (copy). January 24, 1914.

Duke, Polly. "The Case of the Perplexing Post Offices." *Playsure Magazine.* August 1980:25-9.

1850 Census Schedule. Harris County. Compiled by Harris Co. Genealogical Society. N. dat.

Fifth and Sixth Grade Class of the Spring Church of Christ. *The First Fifty Years: A History of Spring Church of Christ.* Spring: Spring Church of Christ. 1987.

Fletcher, Herbert, ed. *Harris County Republic of Texas.* Harris County Historical Society. Houston: Anson Jones Press, 1950.

Goedecke, Rudolph. Personal Interview. Spring, TX. November 12, 2000.

Haude, Diana L. *The Lemm Family.* Spring, TX. May 1982.

"Historic Old Town Spring," *The Old Town Spring News.* Vol 1, Issue 2, January 1984. 1.

Hoffmann, Annie. Personal Interview. Spring, TX. June 10, 1988.

"Hounds Trail Negro Who Shot Spring Officer." *Houston Chronicle.* Thursday, April 15, 1915: 4.

"Houston Northwest: Indian tribes, early settlers make area what it is today. . ." *Houston Suburbia.* Summer 1978: n. pag.

Hudson, Doug. Telephone Interview. Houston, TX. March 9, 2000.

James, Louise B. "Spring, Texas: Little Town for All Seasons." *The Sunday Oklahoman.* Travel Sec., Sunday, October 19, 1986.

The Joyce Gay Report: Old Town Spring. Joyce Gay. J. G. Productions, Houston, TX, 1991.

Karkabi, Barbara. "Spring Cafe claims the best food and slowest service—anywhere," *Houston Chronicle.* Sec. 4. Wednesday, April 11, 1980:n. pag.

Kerber, Sallie Stanley. *The Historical Development of Spring, Texas.* Unpublished research for Historical Geography of the United States 368. Huntsville TX, April 30, 1981.

Kessler, Elizabeth. *In Others' Words: A Narrative Ethnography of Spring, Texas.* Unpublished research. July 1993.

"Kids Come First! in Spring ISD." General Information 1999-2000. Spring Independent School District.

Kimball, Mary Holt, Bicentennial Project Chairman, and Committee. *The Heritage of North Harris County.* Houston: North Harris County Branch, American Association of University Women, 1977.

Laird, Cheryl. "Visiting Old Town Spring," *Texas: Houston Chronicle Magazine.* November 4, 1990:16,18.

McDowell, Leslie. "Spring creek once flowed with canoes, trade." *The 1960 Sun*. May 22, 1996: 1, 5A.

Magill, Jim. "Old-timers to relive bygone days at 'Home for Holidays.'" *Houston Chronicle*. Neighborhood Supplement. Wednesday, October 26, 1988:1.

Mallott, David. "Spring Changing Around Old Mallott Home." *The Spring Tribune*. N. dat:n. pag.

Mallott, Dorothy. Personal Interview. Spring, TX, December 31, 1999.

McGinley, Theresa Kurk. *Just a Whistle Stop Away, The History of Old Town Spring*. Nacogdoches: East Texas Historical Association, 2000.

Meyer, Avalt. Personal Interview. Spring, TX, November 5, 1995.

Meyer, Avalt. Personal Interview. Houston, TX, August 15, 2000.

Mills, Clay. Telephone Interview. Spring, TX. November 9, 2000.

Mr. John A. Winship: In Memoriam. Spring Independent School District archives.

Moore, Maxine and Donnie Caton. "1838-1936: Spring Community is Carved from Wilderness." *The 1960 Sun*. N. dat:n. pag.

"Negro Admits Shooting; He Claims Self-Defense." *Houston Chronicle*. Saturday, April 17, 1916:1.

"Negro Arrested at Livingston." *Houston Chronicle*. Saturday, April 17, 1915:9.

1931 Texas Almanac. N. pub. 1931.

Old Spring Courthouse Museum and Visitor's Center. Unpublished proposal for museum site. 1994. Spring Historical Museum archives.

"Old Town Spring Lives Up to Billing. 'A Town for All Tastes and Seasons.'" *The Old Town Spring Souvenir*. Randy and Linda Woods, pub. Vol. 3, No. 6, June 1999:15.

"$100 Reward is Offered for Negro Slayer." *Houston Chronicle*. Friday, April 16, 1915:19.

Pennington, Lelia. Personal Interview. Spring, TX. November 24, 2000.

Pierson, Sam C., Jr. "Hotel-saloon in Spring celebrates its designation as historic landmark." *Houston Chronicle*. Sec. 1, October 1984:n. pag.

Pittman, Steven. "Teacher helps preserve small Spring Cemetery. *The 1960 Sun*. June 30, 1993: 1,5.

Plats of Town of Spring, Robinson Addition, Sellers Addition, and Kelly Addition. *Assessor's Block Book for Harris County, Texas*. Certified copy, May 11, 1994. Spring Historical Museum archives.

Prescott, Walter Webb, ed. *Handbook of Texas*. Ann Arbor, MI: Edwards Bros, 1976.

"Robbers of Banks Near Houston." *The Houston Post*. Saturday , January 7, 1933:1

"Robert Lee Robinson, Pioneer Spring Resident." N. dat. Spring Historical Museum archives.

Robinson, John. Personal Interview. Spring, TX. November 5, 1995.

Robinson, John. Personal Interview. Houston, TX, September 27, 2000.

Russell Gardens: America's First Name in Daylillies. Spring, TX, 1959.

St. Paul United Methodist: 110 Year Anniversary. Spring, TX: St. Paul United Methodist Church, May 7, 1995.

Salyers, Gertie Mae Duce. Personal Interview. Spring, TX, February 17, 2000.

Salyers, Gertie Mae Duce. Speech at opening of Spring Historical Museum, November 5, 1995.

Schultz, LuAnne Wunsche. Personal Interview. Spring, TX, March 2, 2000.

Sellers, Natalene. Personal Interview. Spring, TX, June 8, 1988.

Seventy-Fifth Anniversary Celebration: Immanuel United Church of Christ. Spring, TX: Immanuel Church, Sunday, July 14, 1991.

Severance, Diana Walzel. *Deep Roots, Strong Branches: A History of the Klein Family and Klein Community 1840-1940*. San Antonio: Historical Publishing Network, 1999.

Severance, Diana Walzel. "Spring, Texas." *The Handbook of Texas Online*. The Texas State Historical Association. February 15, 1999. (http://www.tsha. utexas.edu/ handbook/online/articles view/SS/ble/eqr 74 html).

"Shot Constable Because Negro Did Not Want to go to Jail." *Houston Chronicle*. April 18, 1915:3.

"Significant Dates in the Development of the Spring Community." Time Line. Spring Historical Museum.

"Spring Cafe Links Town to Busy Railroad Past." *Houston Chronicle*. Sunday, September 6, 1970: n. pag.

Spring Cemetery: Research and Historical Marker Documentation by North Harris College Honors Students and Faculty. September 19, 2000.

Spring Cemetery. Unpublished proposal submitted to Harris County Historical Commission. Spring Historical Museum archives.

Spring Chamber of Commerce letter. 1926. Spring Historical Museum archives.

"Spring Creek County." *Montgomery County History*. Conroe: Harris County Genealogical Society, 1981.

"Spring ISD reflects on 50 years of education, faces challenge of future." *Spring Times*. Vol. 10, No. 3: March 1985. 1-2.

Spring Post Offices. Notes and documents. Spring Historical Museum archives.

Summation and Records of Land Conveyance. J. C. Sellers, 1906, 1907, 1912, 1923

Deed from J. C. Sellers to C. G. Barrett, October 4, 1906, (filed December 28, 1906) Harris Co., Deed Records, vol. 198:55.

Deed from J. C. Sellers to M. B. Harper, November 20, 1906, (filed June 12, 1908), Harris Co., Deed Records, vol. 220:3.

Deed from J. C. Sellers to Paul Mueschke, January 7, 1907, (filed January 6, 1908), Harris Co., Deed Records, vol. 214:23.

Deed from J. C. Sellers to C. G. Barrett, August 15, 1907, (filed September 4, 1907), Harris Co., Deed Records, n. vol., n. pag.

Deed from J. C. Sellers to Trustees Spring Independent School District, December 19, 1907, (filed December 26, 1907), Harris Co., n. vol., n. page.

Deed from J. C. Sellers to K. C. Bell, October 23, 1912, n. file dat., Harris Co., n. vol., n. pag.

Deed from J. C. Sellers to the Colored Peoples of Spring, Texas, and their heirs, July 31, 1923, (filed May 23, 1935), Harris Co., Deed Records, vol. 855:711.

Theiss, Karl, Jr. Telephone Interview. Spring, TX. May 19, 2000.

Theiss, Lydia. Telephone Interview. Spring, TX. June 30, 2000.

Thoms, Norma Boggs. Letter to Spring Historical Museum. Carmel, CA. July 22, 1996.

Thurmann, Ila. Telephone Interview. Spring, TX, June 1995.

Thurmann, Shirley. Personal Interview. Spring, TX. November 24, 2000

Title Run Sheets. Town of Spring. Robinson Addition. Kelly Addition. Sellers Addition. Records from c. 1861 to c. 1970. (copy)

Truevine Missionary Baptist Church Celebrates 93 Years. Spring, TX: Truevine Baptist Church, November 12, 1995.

Tullos, Gladys Hildebrandt. *A German Family Contributes to the Development of Spring: My Family Heritage.* Unpublished Manuscript. March 10, 1986, Spring Independent School District archives.

Vaughan, Jesse L., Jr. *The Holzwarth/Holzworth Family: Wurttemberg, Germany and Galveston and Harris Counties, Texas ca. A. D. 1600 to present.* No publisher:n. dat.

Veteto, Bob. "Spring Cafe Grew Out of Railroaders' Thirst." *Spring Tribune.* Vol. 2, No. 16, Wednesday, August 16. 1972: n. pag.

Weaver, W. W. Telephone Interview. Spring, TX, February 22, 2000.

Wells, Creola. Telephone Interview. Spring, TX, March 2, 2000.

Werner, George C. "Railroads." *The Handbook of Texas Online.* The Texas State Historical Association. February 15, 1999 (http://www.tsha.utexas.edu/handbook/online/articles/view/RR/eqr 1html).

Williams, Edward E. "A Fourth of July in Spring." *Texas: Houston Chronicle Magazine.* July 3, 1988: 6-9.

Wunsche, Irma Goedecke. Telephone Interview. Spring, TX. November 18, 2000.

Wunsche, August. Personal Interview. Spring, TX. June 27, 2000.

HARPER-KLEIN HOME
1897

IMMANUEL EVANGELICAL
AND
REFORMED CHURCH
1916

SPRING STATE
BANK

ROBINSON HOME
1903

SPRING DEPOT

SPRING HISTORICAL SOCIETY

SPRING, TEXAS

SPRING SCHOOL
1921

SPRING
CREEK

WUNSCHE BROS

WUNSCHE BROTHERS
SALOON
1902

SAW MILL

CARL WUNSCHE SR.
HIGH SCHOOL
1939

WILSON-MALLOTT HOME
1898

The Spring Historical Museum features a souvenir afghan for sale at the gift shop. Woven into the afghan are pictures significant to the development of the town of Spring.

The Spring Historical Society and the Spring Historical Museum

The Spring Historical Society, a group which originally formed to preserve the history of the old Carl Wunsche High School and then expanded its horizons, is a body dedicated to researching and collecting historical and genealogical records, folklore, and artifacts of Spring and the surrounding area.

The Society saw its "dream come true" when the Harris County Commissioners' Court gave permission to convert the old Spring courthouse into a museum. The museum is the first to operate under the auspices of Harris County. The museum features exhibits which trace the development of Spring, Texas, from 1840 to the present. On display are pictures of early families that contributed to the town's endurance for almost 150 years. The town's first phone booth; the town wheelchair; photographic presentations which depict early business, schools, and churches; and other memorabilia from earlier days enliven the museum building.

Although not eligible for historic recognition itself, the courthouse building, with its staid facade, has had varied uses since its completion in 1948, having been created originally as a church, then serving as a courthouse, as a meeting place for other churches, and for a brief time , according to some sources, as home to a "hippie commune."

Staffed by volunteers from the local AARP and DAR groups, the museum is open Thursday through Saturday from 10:00 A.M. to 5:00 P.M., and Sunday, 1:00 P.M. to 5:00 P.M. Admission is free. For more information, call 281-651-0055.

Travel back in time: Spend a day in Old Town Spring. Yes, shop at the shops! But don't miss the Spring Historical Museum.

Index